Walks in

HISTORIC LEICESTERSHIRE & RUTLAND

Walks in HISTORIC LEICESTERSHIRE & RUTLAND

BRYAN WAITES

COUNTRYSIDE BOOKS
NEWBURY, BERKSHIRE

First published 2001

COUNTRYSIDE BOOKS
3 Catherine Road
Newbury, Berkshire

To view our complete range of books,
please visit us at
www.countrysidebooks.co.uk

ISBN 1 85306 681 8

Designed by Graham Whiteman
Photographs by Beryl Waites
Maps by the author and redrawn by
Jennie Collins
Front cover photographs supplied by Bill Meadows

Produced through MRM Associates Ltd., Reading
Printed by J. W. Arrowsmith Ltd., Bristol
Typeset by Techniset Typesetters, Newton-le-Willows

This book is dedicated to the memory
of two great Yorkshiremen:
Trevor Wilson, a very dear friend for 45 years
and F.R. Pearson, my inspiring history teacher.

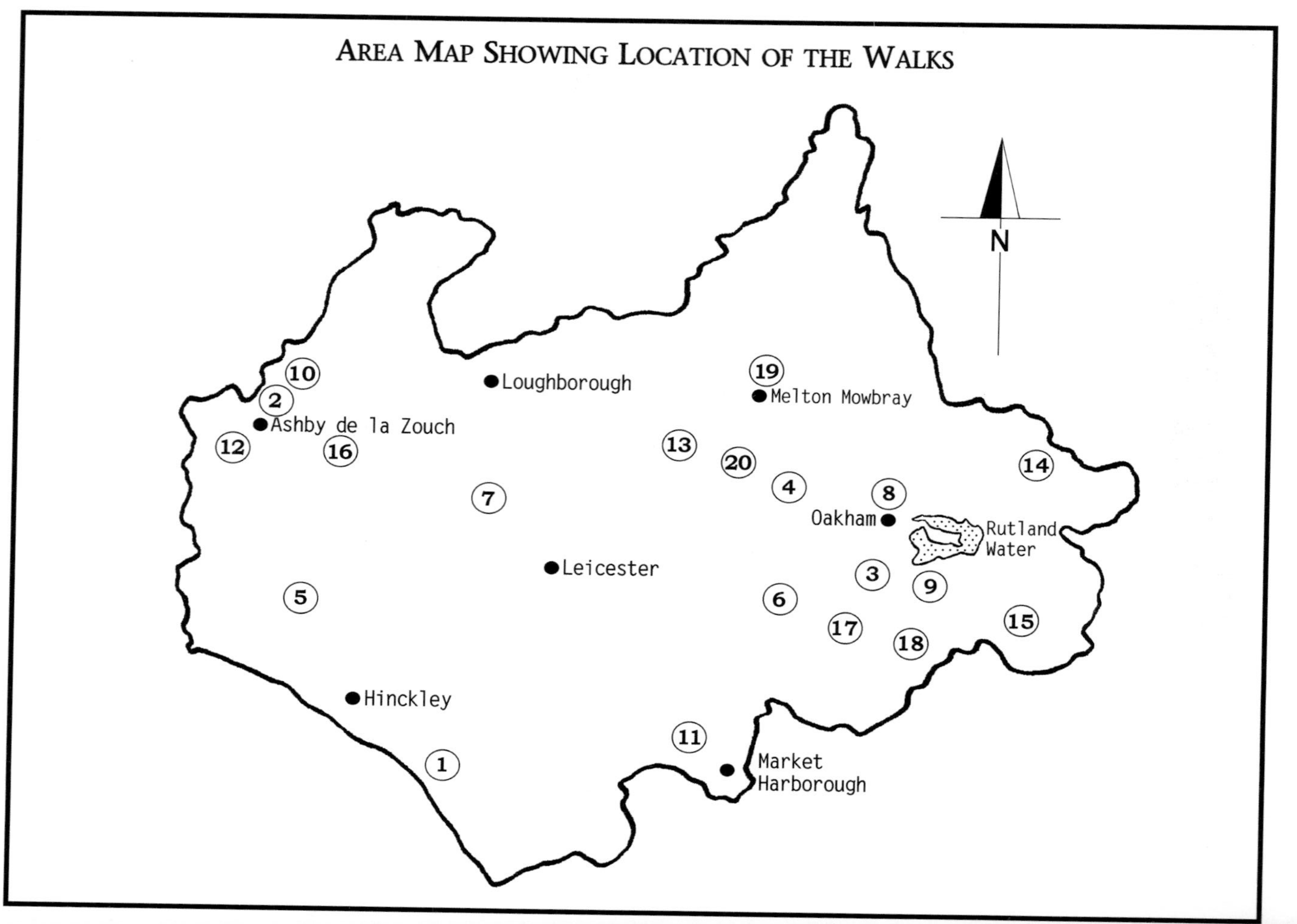
AREA MAP SHOWING LOCATION OF THE WALKS
N
Loughborough
Melton Mowbray
Ashby de la Zouch
Oakham
Rutland Water
Leicester
Hinckley
Market Harborough
1
2
3
4
5
6
7
8
9
10
11
12
13
14
15
16
17
18
19
20

Contents

WALK

PUBLISHER'S NOTE

We hope that you obtain considerable enjoyment from this book; great care has been taken in its preparation. Although at the time of publication all routes followed public rights of way or permitted paths, diversion orders can be made and permissions withdrawn.

We cannot of course be held responsible for such diversion orders and any inaccuracies in the text which result from these or any other changes to the routes nor any damage which might result from walkers trespassing on private property. We are anxious though that all details covering the walks are kept up to date and would therefore welcome information from readers which would be relevant to future editions.

INTRODUCTION

History is all around us if we care to see it and know about it. As the popular historian W.G. Hoskins wrote, 'The English landscape is the richest historical record we possess'. He saw the need for 'laborious scrambling on foot wherever the trail may lead', as a necessity to understanding and enjoyment.

His interpretation of landscape was all inclusive – countryside, fields, farms, settlements, woodland and marsh, buildings, country houses and stately homes, roads, railways, canals, towns, and cities – and much more. We have to remember people also for as Ratzel, the German geographer wrote, 'a people expresses itself through its landscape'.

A landscape without figures may be felt as a presence, but in the end it is the people who ultimately give life, vivacity and meaning to it. Landscape without people is a skeleton without flesh.

With this in mind, these history walks have been chosen to illustrate personalities mainly. There are only three exceptions – following a Roman road, finding a lost village and marvelling at an engineering miracle. Here the landscape reveals its secrets.

Otherwise we look for the places which have associations with personalities – some well known like Richard III and John Clare, others not so well known, like Thomas Barker, 'Father of English Meteorology' and Edward Thring – a great headmaster. One walk is associated with a fictional hero – Ivanhoe.

The walks represent history from Roman times to the 1930s. They cover the counties of Leicestershire and Rutland and, indeed, if space allowed, there are many more famous links, which might have been included, for the surprising discovery is that even the smallest and most remote place has some person or something of note about it.

The 20 walks in themselves are for the family and vary in length from 2 miles to 6½ miles. Generally they are over level or undulating land (but be ready occasionally for boggy, uneven sections) and frequently well waymarked (though there are still some exceptions). Wear walking boots; take binoculars if you can, dress according to the weather. Picnics are possible on many walks, though in all instances there is a pub or tea room nearby. Please park with care in villages, as it does matter so much to the residents. If you park at a pub please make sure you have permission. Respect the countryside code and always have the book and map handy. Three walks are in towns –

Oakham, Uppingham and Melton Mowbray, so you may not need walking boots etc there.

In each place there is something to see, ranging from a museum or castle to a medieval deer park and a lime kiln. All will evoke the memory and association, which is the chosen theme of the walk.

If you need more details about pubs, museums, opening times, facilities etc the telephone numbers have been given. Directions on how to get to your walk are provided and places of interest nearby mentioned also. Most walks can be done in a morning, afternoon or summer evening. Some can be combined for a good day out – for example John Clare at Pickworth and Thomas Cook at Barrowden. A list of further references has been given if you wish to extend your interest in a particular person or place.

Sketch maps are included to give you an overview of the route to be taken but you will inevitably find more detail if you use the relevant Ordnance Survey map. The smaller scale OS Landranger (1:50,000) covers a wider area but the new OS Explorer (1:25,000) has more detail and is the better map for walkers.

I am especially grateful to the following people and publications: Leicester Museum, Arts & Record Services; Anthony Squires; Rodney Lines and Tim Clough for their articles in *Rutland Record,* Nos 12, 13 and 18; to John Kington's *Weather Journals of a Rutland Squire*; and Joyce Lee's *Who's Buried Where in Leicestershire*; to David Carlin; to Mrs B Keene and Mr R Weatherby; NW Leicestershire District Council; to Beryl Waites and Dr Gillian Dawson for companionship and advice on the walks, to Beryl for the photographs also, and to Gillian for help in processing the manuscript. We enjoyed the walks and learnt a great deal. Not only that, but we hope they kept us fit and alert. We wish the same joy and benefits to you.

Bryan Waites

WALK 1

FOLLOWING A ROMAN ROAD – HIGH CROSS AND THE FOSSE WAY

Length: $5\frac{1}{2}$ miles

The Almshouses, Frolesworth

HOW TO GET THERE: From the A5 turn off at High Cross following signs to Claybrooke Magna and Frolesworth. About 1 mile out of Frolesworth on the Sharnford road turn left at the minor crossroads. The Fosse Meadows Nature Park is $\frac{1}{2}$ mile along on the right.

PARKING: The car park at Fosse Meadow Nature Park.

MAP: OS Landranger 140 Leicester & Coventry area (GR 491911).

Introduction

High Cross was regarded as the centre of Roman England and is marked by an 18th century pillar. Watling Street, from London to Chester, crossed the Fosse Way, from Exeter to Lincoln, at this point. They still do, and you can have a walk along one of the best surviving sections which remains, north east of High Cross.

Although your walk along the Fosse Way will be a gentle stroll in a leafy lane, you will suddenly find yourself at a good vantage point when you reach High Cross. Here you see the beautiful heart of south-west Leicestershire that is bounded for miles by Watling Street acting as the county line. The walk takes you more deeply into this via Claybrooke Magna and Frolesworth and the small streams you may see and cross are the headwaters of the river Soar flowing eventually to the Trent and then the Humber estuary. In fact, you will be walking very close to one of the major watersheds in England, with streams like the Swift and Avon to the south flowing to the Severn; the Welland flowing to the Wash as well as the Soar northwards to the Trent. Perhaps being on top of the world, English style, both historically and geographically, will make you feel even more invigorated than usual!

History

The Fosse Way was constructed about AD45 and ran from Lincoln to Bath and Exeter. It was virtually straight for 200 miles. The stretch from Stoney Bridge to High Cross is one of the few sections to survive in the original form. At one time the Fosse Way marked the frontier in Roman Britain. It rises gently to High Cross on Watling Street, the most important Roman road in Britain running from London to Chester, reaching 443 ft above sea level. Using your maps, it is interesting to note that the Fosse Way has been used throughout history to mark boundaries and you will find many parish, district and county boundaries follow this line.

The Place

High Cross is about 13 miles from the other High Cross in the centre of Leicester. The Fosse Way made its way to the town, crossing the river Soar and then aiming for Willoughby-on-the-Wolds before crossing the Trent at Newark and then arriving in Lincoln. A significant Roman settlement called Venonis was located at High Cross and many finds have been made, though as yet no major dig has taken place here. Keep your eyes open in the fields and along the Fosse Way, you may be lucky enough to find a tile, coin or pottery.

High Cross monument, Fosse Way

THE WALK

❶ Turn right leaving the car park, passing Cottage Farm on your right. The surfaced road bends left to Claybrooke Lodge Farm but you carry on ahead to the rough track with a footpath sign. There is no difficulty following the Fosse Way as it goes to High Cross and the distance is about 2 miles. You will pass through several kissing gates and the track becomes narrow in places but it is very attractive with shady, arched tree-lined sections. To each side you will glimpse, from time to time, arable and pasture fields and about halfway through there is Sharnford Lodge Farm on your right. If you observe the track very carefully you will see a cobbled surface and ditches at the sides. In some places the track is raised above field level, especially noticeable to your right. There are excellent views to the south and south-east. Look for the tower of Frolesworth church.

❷ As you reach the main road you will find a very helpful information board giving details of the Fosse Way, on your right. If you turn right here and go a short distance down Bumble Bee Lane you will come to the lovely High Cross Guest House on your left. Just next to this is the High Cross monument. Now return to the information board to read about it and then proceed left down the hill into Claybrooke Magna on the B577, 1 mile away. The welcoming sign of the Pig in Muck comes into view and you can call in for a pint in the garden behind the inn. Take the road on the left for Frolesworth and in ½ mile you cross a stream which is one of the river Soar's most distant tributaries. There is a notice on your right 'Claybrooke Mill: Agricultural Merchants & Flour Millers'. A little further on you will see a footpath sign on your left at an iron gate.

❸ Go onto the path keeping to the left of the hedge. Look for the signs and yellow markers all along this part of the route. In the far right-hand corner of the field cross a stile (marker) then in a few hundred yards, another stile. Keep to the left following a wooden fence and aim for the corner of the pasture field with a stile and sign attached. Cross the stile on the left to yellow marker posts. Next go over a stile and plank bridge which leads into a

HOSTELRY AND THIRSTQUENCHER

The Pig in Muck in Claybrooke Magna is a lively place with pub snacks, traditional ales, guest beers, SkyTV, live entertainment, skittles and pub games. Telephone: 01455 209248. The Plough and Harrow at Frolesworth offers hot and cold food, Tetleys and Carlsberg. Telephone: 01455 209139. Both have big car parks.

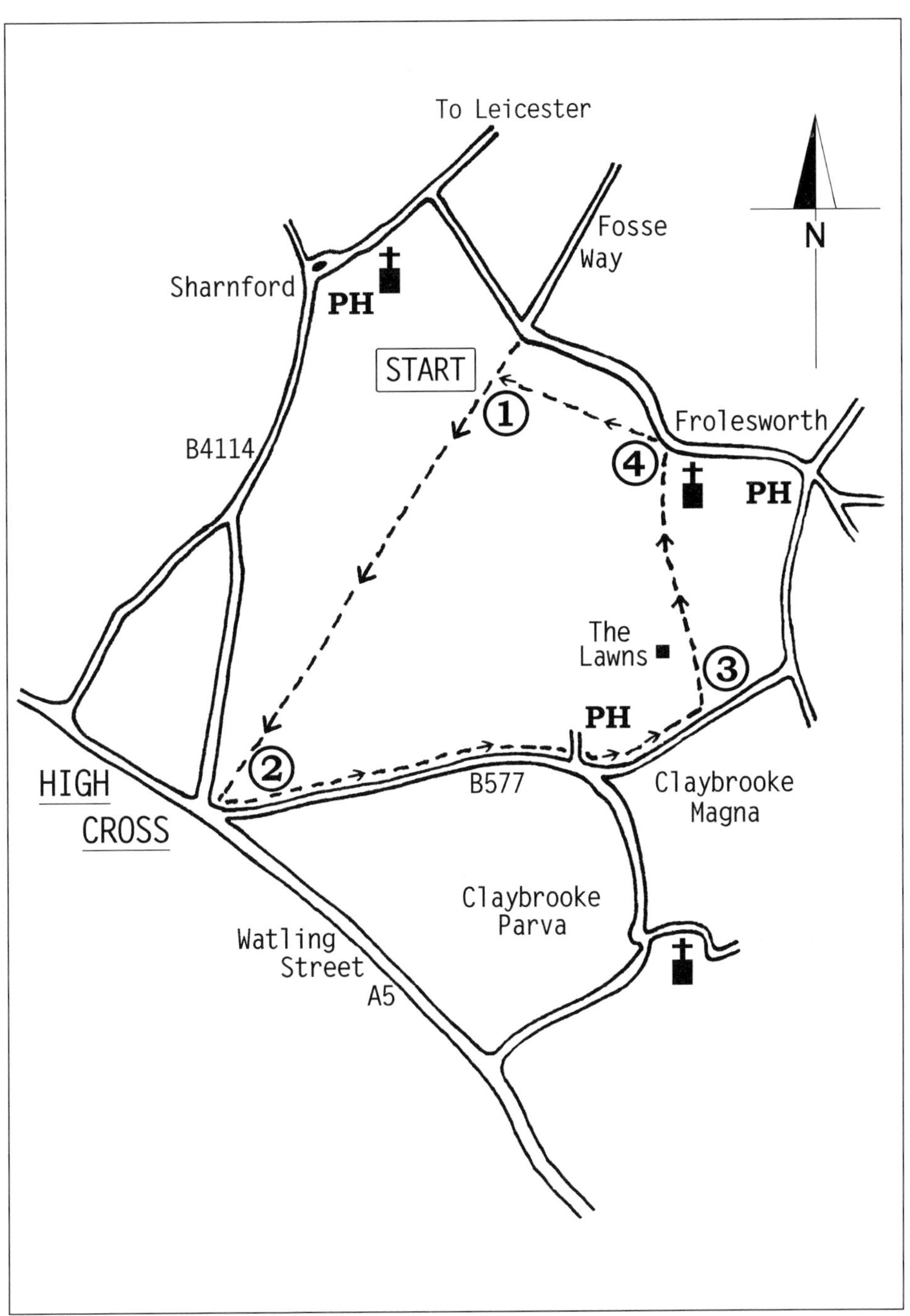
To Leicester
Fosse Way
N
Sharnford
PH
START
1
Frolesworth
B4114
4
PH
The Lawns
3
PH
2
HIGH CROSS
B577
Claybrooke Magna
Claybrooke Parva
Watling Street
A5

pasture field. Cross the field diagonally towards the white house (The Lawns) on the hill top. Go through a small metal gate leading to the drive and close to the house. Excellent views if you look back to the Claybrookes.

Turn right, crossing a cattle grid, along the drive for 100 yards to a stile in the wire fence on your left. Cross into the pasture field to a yellow marker post with Frolesworth ahead, ½ mile away. Go on to a plank bridge and stile in the hedge opposite, and enjoy the good views to the north-west. Keeping to the hedge on your left, cross rough pasture to the corner ahead. Climb double stiles with a plank bridge then go diagonally as indicated by arrows with a large duck pond on your left. Go over to the marked stile in the hedge opposite. At the double stile cross and again go diagonally right through the field towards the bungalows on the skyline, aiming for a yellow marker post at the far side.

OTHER PLACES OF INTEREST

Burbage Common and woods, off the B4668 east of Hinckley, display spectacular ground flora. Telephone. 01455 633712. Mill-on-the-Soar Falconry and Fishing Centre, Coventry Road, Sutton in the Elms offers flying demonstrations by owls, hawks, falcons and buzzards, and has a fishing lake. Telephone. 01455 285924.

❹ You emerge on a grassy track between two fields. Turn right to the village of Frolesworth with one final look back over the landscape you have covered. Bear left on the track, with the church well to your right, between houses on to the main street of the village with White Cottage opposite. You may want to spend some time looking round the church and village. However, to continue your walk, remember to turn left with White Cottage opposite you and in 100 yards you come to a footpath sign at a farm entrance. Go down a concrete drive and cross a very rough pasture field. Aim for a gap in the hedge opposite, to the right of an ash tree. Cross a low fence and plank bridge into an arable field. Go across the middle of this field to the far side. If a crop is growing a path is usually easily visible through it. Look back for a view of Frolesworth on a terrace above river levels. Keep straight on, crossing another arable field to a gap in the large tree forming part of a line of trees in front of you, which is the Fosse Way. Much of the time you will see a green barn and a red-roofed house diagonally to your right. Exit the final field at a gap leading onto the Fosse Way. There is a sign here 'Public Footpath to Frolesworth' pointing back along your route. Turn left, over the small bridge, and then right into your car park.

WALK 2
IVANHOE AND ASHBY DE LA ZOUCH CASTLE

Length: 2½ miles

Ashby Castle

HOW TO GET THERE: The A511 leads to Ashby from both east and west.

PARKING: The car park at North Street, at present free. It is near the Tourist Information Centre.

MAP: OS Landranger 128 Derby and Burton-upon-Trent (GR 361167). Ask at the Tourist Centre for a street map.

INTRODUCTION

Authors and their fictional characters can make an area famous; Bronte country, Hardy's Wessex and Catherine Cookson country are well known. Because Sir Walter Scott set the tournament in *Ivanhoe* at Ashby de la Zouch

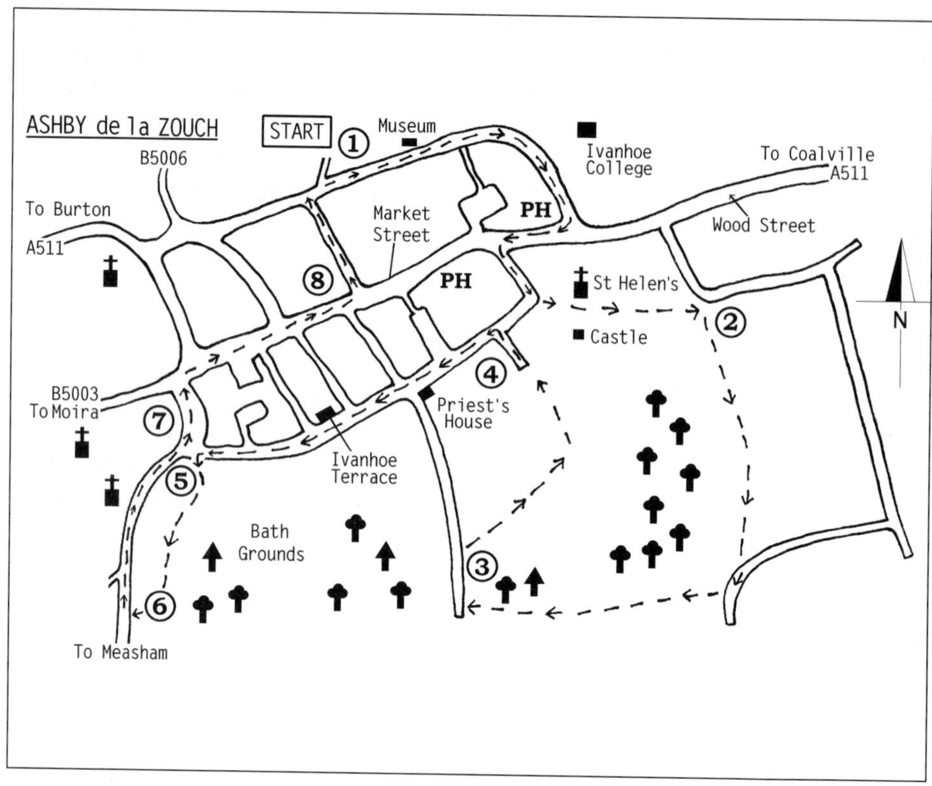

Castle, the reputation of this ancient town has also been enhanced. This is a fascinating walk through history, visiting the castle and exploring Ashby's historic streets.

History

Ashby Castle is one of the most impressive in the Midlands, yet it was originally a Norman manor house, later converted to a fortress by Lord Hastings in the 15th century. The magnificent tower was built in 1464 and gives excellent views around. As the castle was meant to resist a siege it was self-contained and had an underground passage linking the tower and the kitchens. During the Civil War the Royalists were besieged by the Roundheads, eventually surrendering after one year. Later, partial destruction was ordered, the Hastings family moved away, and the castle fell into ruin and was forgotten. Largely as a result of the popularity of Sir Walter Scott's novel *Ivanhoe* (1819) the castle was preserved and is now in the care of English

Heritage. Scott's hero is Wilfred of Ivanhoe, who served with King Richard in the Crusades but returns to England to find much oppression under Prince John, the King's brother. In disguise, Ivanhoe fights in the tournament at Ashby Castle and defeats the knights of Prince John, including the Templar, Sir Brian de Bois-Guilbert. Locksley, alias Robin Hood, also features in the story, which continues with the wounded Ivanhoe eventually being chosen as champion for Rebecca, the Jewess, in a Trial by Combat. Jousting tournaments are still held in the castle grounds, along with many other events.

THE PLACE

St Helen's church was built in the 15th century on the site of an earlier church, also by Lord Hastings. The stained glass and heraldic glass are outstanding as, too, the Hastings monuments. Along the walk you see evidence of the Spa Town and Ivanhoe Terrace, which flourished in the 19th century. Market Street is full of character and interest with medieval timber-framed, Georgian and modern buildings. Ashby Castle is open April to September daily 10 am to 6 pm; October daily 10 am to 4 pm; November to March (Wednesday to Sunday) 10 am to 4 pm. Closed for lunch 1 pm to 2 pm daily. Telephone: 01530 413343. Ashby Museum, North Street opens Easter to September weekdays 10 am to 12 noon; 2 pm to 4 pm. Saturday 10 am to 4 pm; Sunday 2 pm to 4 pm. Telephone: 01530 560090.

THE WALK

❶ Start at the free car park in North Street. The Tourist Information Centre and Museum are nearby. Go along to the end of this street noting Ivanhoe College, and at the road junction cross carefully into Lower Church Street opposite. Walk to St Helen's church at the end, into the churchyard and follow the path until it reaches Mount Walk.

❷ Turn right into Mount Walk, which fringes Ashby Castle. When this reaches the main road, Upper Packington Road, turn right into Prior Park. Follow this lane until you reach a road, Prior Park Road. Turn right and in a short distance you see a gap in the hedge on the right.

HOSTELRY AND THIRSTQUENCHER

There are several teashops, pubs and restaurants in and around Market Street. The White Hart is an impressive 18th/19th century building once the 'bawdiest public house in the Midlands'. See the bear pit inside. Did Dick Turpin stop here? Telephone: 01530 414531. Also, the Fayre & Firkin (once The Bull's Head) is reputed to be the oldest house in Ashby. Telephone: 01530 412653.

Jousting tournaments are held in the castle grounds

❸ Go through this gap into the cricket field, cross to the brick ruined tower at the far corner. Turn left along a wide track with excellent views of the castle. The entrance is here if you wish to go in.

❹ At South Street turn left and continue to the end where you reach the impressive Our Lady of Lourdes Roman Catholic church, Holy Trinity church and the Loudoun Monument. As you come down South Street look for the Priest's House on your left and Ivanhoe Terrace on your right. You might also note house names such as Ivanhoe, Rowena, and Wilfred Place is nearby.

❺ Turn left opposite the monument and go into the park, once Bath Grounds, now Hastings Gardens. Follow the path through the park and then onto Station Road. In the park, on your right, you will see the site of Ivanhoe Baths, once an integral part of the Spa Town.

❻ If you wish you could turn left and go to see the old station building, carefully restored in the

OTHER PLACES OF INTEREST

Ashby is in the heart of the National Forest and the Visitor Centre is just minutes away. The renowned Saxon sculpture and marvellous view at Breedon, a little along the A453 from Ashby, should be seen.

1980s, now offices, and the remains of the track of the 1849 railway. Otherwise, turn right to pass the Royal Hotel and Rawdon Terrace, also part of the hey-day of the Spa Town, which was encouraged by the publicity and popularity of Scott's *Ivanhoe.*

❼ Carry on into Bath Street and Market Street noting the fine buildings such as the Town Hall and Market, the White Hart, the Fayre & Firkin, and at the far end, St Helen's House and No 108.

❽ Now return to the car park via Mill Lane, which has been carefully restored and contains a delightful row of period shops. This is one of many tiny lanes, which run off Market Street.

WALK 3
FINDING A LOST VILLAGE – MARTINSTHORPE

Length: 5 miles

A desirable residence in Martinsthorpe?

HOW TO GET THERE: From Oakham take the A6003 to Uppingham and turn left at the Manton sign, 3 miles out of Oakham. Then turn first left down a lane to the Horse and Jockey.

PARKING: Outside the Horse and Jockey or along the approach lane.

MAP: OS Explorer 15 Rutland Water & Stamford (GR 878046).

Introduction

Between Oakham and Uppingham in Rutland there are a series of ridges and valleys. Small streams run west to east and when the sun shines the red soils of Rutland are highlighted in the arable fields, particularly on the ridge tops. On the Martinsthorpe ridge there are wonderful views towards Rutland Water and Burley House on the skyline. All around, as you look, you will see church spires and villages within a few miles but mostly you will feel a sense of space and isolation here. This is enhanced by a solitary building in a field, which is all that remains of the former village of Martinsthorpe. This walk will take you into the land of the lost. You will find villages fossilised into the landscape if you know where to look.

History

Martinsthorpe is a deserted village. Only one building remains on the site amidst what appears to be a jumble of earthworks. The location is impressive, on the north-facing slope of a ridge with views all around. The settlement was first mentioned in 1199 and in 1327 there were 14 householders – a village population of about 70. The Fielding family became the Earls of Denbigh in 1622 and built a mansion at Martinsthorpe, which was demolished in 1755, except the chapel, and the stables were turned into a house. For many years this was a shepherd's house but it is now dilapidated. The last person to be born in this house was a Mrs Spink who died in March 1978. Parts of the old chapel could be seen in 1908 but now only a small mound marks its site.

Apart from Martinsthorpe you will also need to look for Gunthorpe lost village which is close to Gunthorpe Hall on the opposite side of the valley. In fact if you could go down the Gwash valley which divides the former villages, you would find several more lost villages, one drowned by the creation of Rutland Water, others, like Normanton, lost due to the emparking activities of a great lord in the 18th century. Halfway round the walk you will find the remarkable village of Brooke with its unique church, growing, it seems from the ground, more like a natural feature than a man-made one. Once there was a flourishing priory nearby and there are many earthworks to show how the landscape changed due to the priory. Also, the village was much bigger. The version you see now is a shrunken one.

The land slopes down towards the river Gwash, north of the Martinsthorpe site and there is a bridge linking Gunthorpe to Martinsthorpe. It is likely that there was a mill hereabouts in medieval times. Also, the main road between Oakham and Uppingham may have passed through the two villages and across the river here. Certainly the road has changed course during the last 500 years. One reason for the desertion of both villages may have been the change of course of the main road, though more likely is the usual depopulation due to either emparking or enclosure for sheep pasture.

The Place

The plan or layout of the former village of Martinsthorpe can be seen on the ground. Near the chapel mound another mound represents the mansion, Martinsthorpe House, and to the south there are traces of the gardens and terraces. North of the existing building is a large square enclosure with ditches, which is believed to have been the old manor house of medieval times. The village road can be detected as a hollow way with signs of house foundations to the side. Outside the boundary wall, which now encloses the village, you can see the ridge and furrow of the old open fields.

The Walk

❶ Start at the Horse and Jockey. Go up the lane to the Manton road. Turn

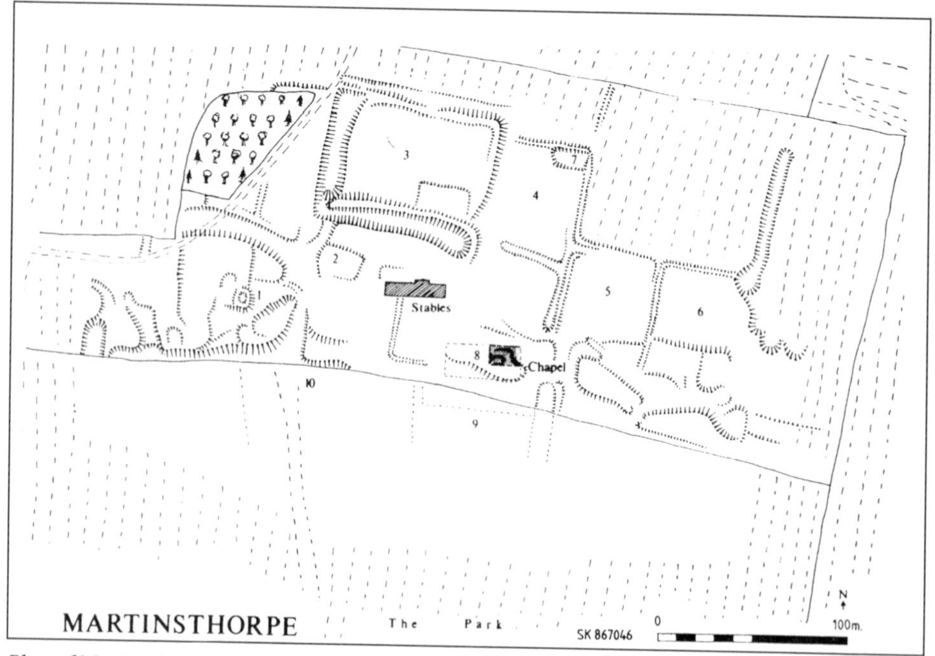

Plan of Martinsthorpe village (courtesy Leicestershire Museums)

St Peter's church, Brooke

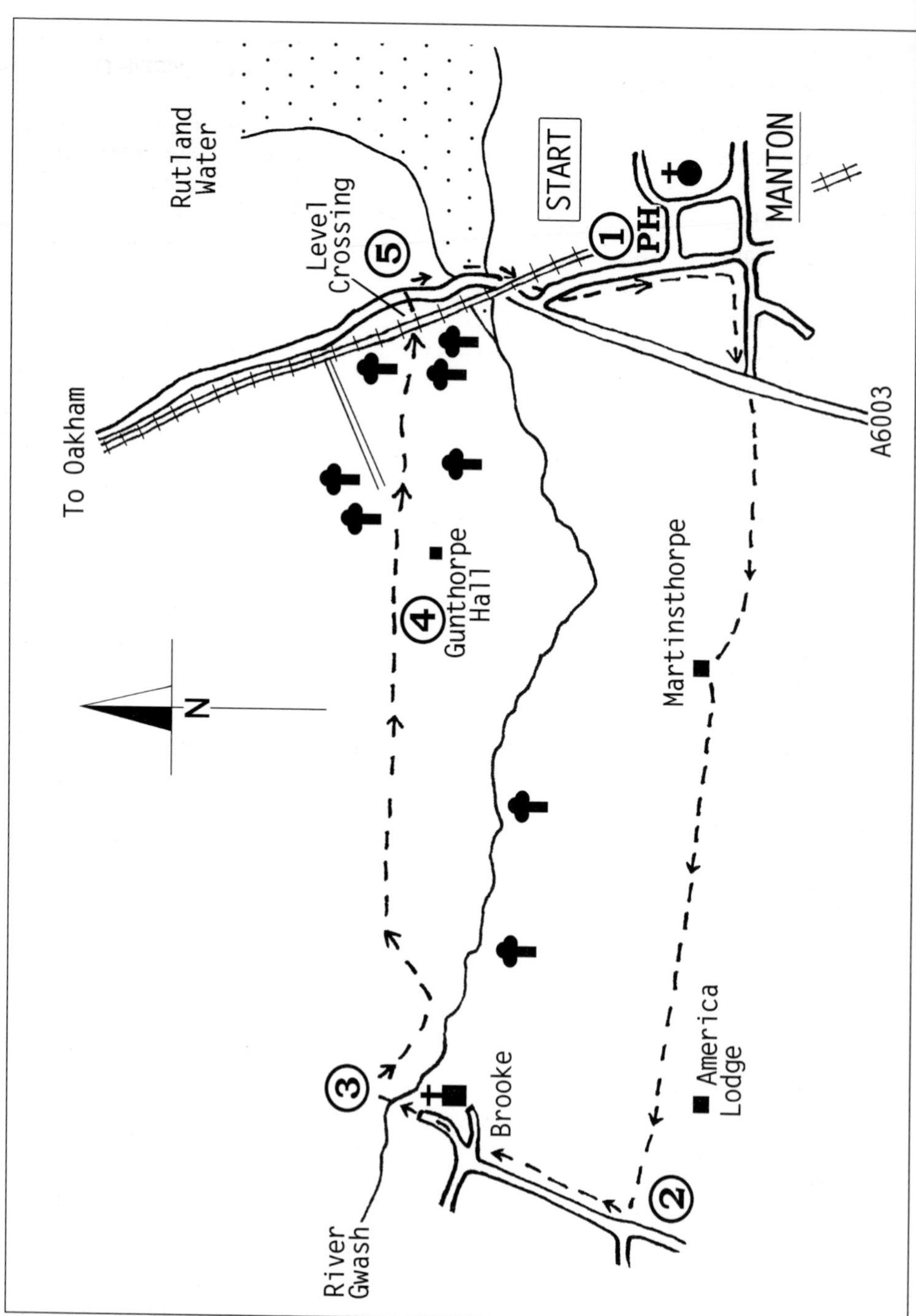
Rutland Water
START
MANTON
PH
1
Level Crossing
5
To Oakham
A6003
4
Gunthorpe Hall
Martinsthorpe
N
3
Brooke
America Lodge
2
River Gwash

right to the A6003. Opposite you there is a farm track on the far side of the dual carriageway. Cross the road very carefully into this track. The path is very clear between hedges and then across a field. Go through a large gate and follow the double line of hawthorns to your left. Cross the field to a gate in the stone wall of the next field. As you enter this field you will see an isolated and empty building surrounded by undulations in the ground. This is the deserted village of Martinsthorpe. Pass the building and make for the pylon a short distance away. You will reach a concrete track leading to a cattle grid. Carry on along until you pass a track on the left to America Lodge. For the next ½ mile the track has a good surface.

HOSTELRY AND THIRSTQUENCHER

The Horse and Jockey pub at Manton is popular with cyclists and walkers. It serves good home-cooked food, snacks and larger meals. Real ales are on offer. Telephone: 01572 737335.

❷ You now reach the road between Brooke and Ridlington. Turn right, walking downhill for ½ mile until you arrive at Brooke. Turn right and pass the church on your right, bearing left down a farm track passing houses and a farm on your left.

❸ Go over a bridge, which crosses the river Gwash, and then turn sharp right into a grass track with hedges on both sides. This is a bridleway and should be signposted. You come to a gate and can enter a field walking to the left side uphill. At the top follow alongside another hedge, keeping it to your left, until you reach a large gap into the next field. Go through the gap and keep to the left of the hedge. Soon you will come to a concrete track leading uphill over a cattle grid. As the track bears left you must go straight on with a wood on your right to a large wooden gate.

❹ You pass a house and stables on your left and reach a drive. Turn right and then sharp left on the drive past a horse chestnut tree in the middle of a triangular patch and also behind Gunthorpe Hall. Soon you pass a sign and come to a double iron gate to your right. Go through and follow a grass track past cottages on your left. Ahead, a wood curves

OTHER PLACES OF INTEREST

Lyndon Hill Visitor Centre and Nature Reserve (Telephone: 01572 737378) and Anglian Water Bird Watching Centre (Telephone: 01572 770651) are both on Rutland Water within 1 mile of Manton.

round the field. Walk all the way round the edge of the wood to the far corner. Here you will have to look carefully for a partially obscured path through the wood. This leads into a small field and you will see a level crossing over a railway for the use of walkers. Look very cautiously in both directions before crossing and in a few yards you are on the A6003.

❺ Cross over with great care to the wide verge on the far side. Walk along to the right and in three minutes you will reach signs showing the Rutland Water cycle circuit. Follow this track under the railway bridge then turn left at a small gate on to the old road, which was superseded by the later by-pass. In 500 yards of uphill walking you will arrive at the Horse and Jockey and your parking place.

WALK 4
AN OUTLAW IN THE ROYAL FOREST – FLITTERIS AND COLD OVERTON PARKS

Length: 4 miles

Bleak House

HOW TO GET THERE: From Oakham and the A606 follow signs to Knossington. From the A47 take the B6047 turning off to Knossington as signposted.

PARKING: Sensible parking in Knossington village.

MAPS: OS Explorer 15 Rutland Water & Stamford (GR 802087).

INTRODUCTION

A peaceful walk amongst the lovely rolling hills of western Rutland, between the villages of Braunston and Knossington, where runs the thousand year old county boundary dividing Rutland from Leicestershire. Partly delineated by this boundary you will find Cold Overton Park Wood and Flitteris Park. Both were once medieval deer parks in the royal forest.

HISTORY

Once, a great royal forest extended from Rockingham Castle in the south to Rutland in the north. In this area it was called the King's Forest of Leighfield. Cold Overton and Flitteris were at its northern extremity. The former was established about 1220 and the latter in 1250. They were subject to strict forest laws administered by forest wardens. The first known warden of the royal forest of Leighfield was Hasculf of Alexton in 1130. This office remained in the family until the 1300s, but one of the family, Peter de Neville, went too far. A document of 1269 shows three pages of his misdemeanours - from false imprisonment to extorting fines and tolls, keeping 300 pigs in the forest, taking 7,000 trees, damaging brushwood, and burning charcoal (illegally). He seized land and for 20 years had pocketed rents that were not his. All these offences against the King were added to by taking animals illegally and imprisoning people wrongly. Eventually, he was declared an outlaw and his lands seized. He may have been hanged in the 1270s. Thus ended the astonishing career of one of Rutland's most versatile villains.

THE PLACE

As you walk between and around the deer parks today – quiet and serene – you may ponder on the activities of these personalities of the past in and around this one time royal forest. You will still find evidence of the ditch and bank that enclosed them and kept in the deer – which were strictly reserved for the king's hunting.

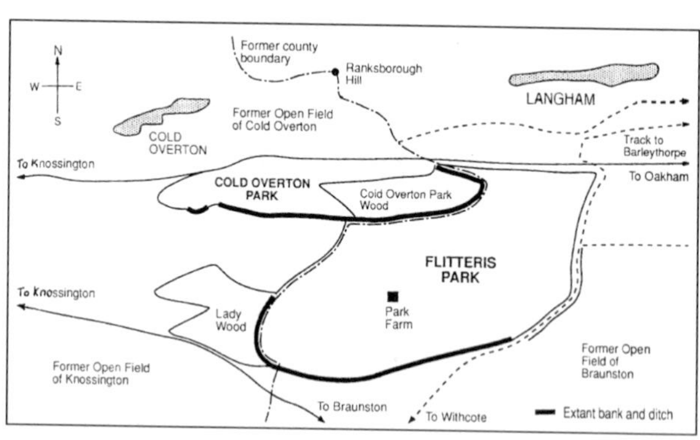

The deer parks of Cold Overton and Flitteris Park (courtesy Rutland Record Society)

The beauty and charm of the Leicestershire countryside

THE WALK

❶ Start at the Fox and Hounds. Walk down Main Street bearing left to the Methodist chapel. Just beyond is The Hollow. Walk down The Hollow. Where the lane forks take the right fork at the footpath sign. Go up the drive to Bleak House but cross the stile a little before the gateway to the house. Go ahead to the marker post to the right of the pond.

HOSTELRY AND THIRSTQUENCHER

The Fox and Hounds at Knossington serves an excellent range of food and drink including Courage real ales and home-made fare, bar snacks as well as main meals. Telephone: 01664 454676. There is also Gates Tea Room at Cold Overton. Telephone: 01664 454309.

❷ Cross the stile and plank bridge here then go ahead uphill to double stiles at the far side of the field. Carry on ahead at the side of the field and continue over a series of stiles following the marker posts

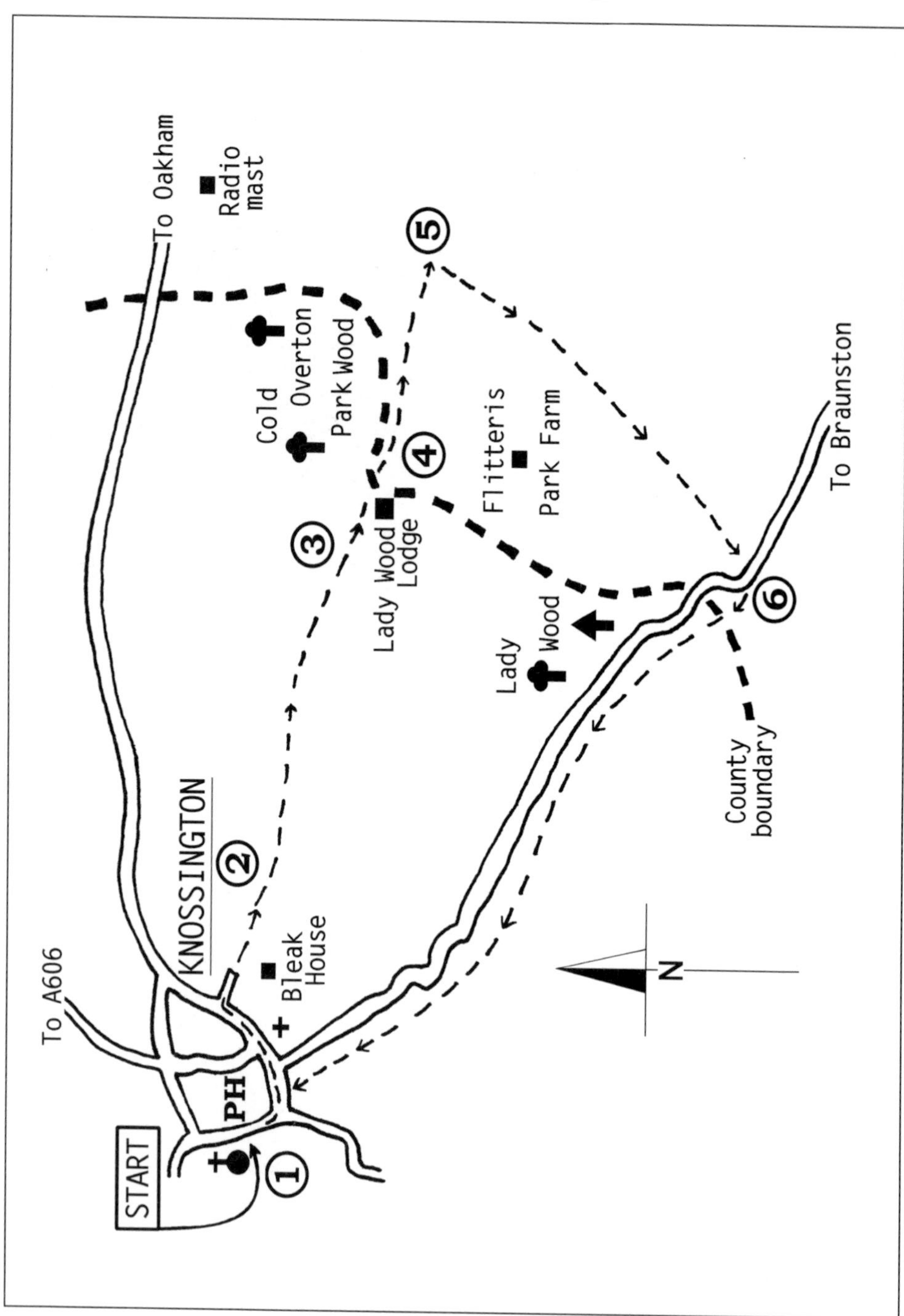
To Oakham
Radio mast
Cold Overton Park Wood
5
4
3
Lady Wood Lodge
Flitteris Park Farm
To Braunston
6
Lady Wood
County boundary
KNOSSINGTON
2
Bleak House
To A606
PH
START
1
N

until you reach the field next to Lady Wood Lodge. This is very clear in front of you.

OTHER PLACES OF INTEREST

Halstead House Farm, Tilton, has farm animals and a nature trail, a tea room and garden centre, a museum, pony rides etc. Telephone: 0116 259 7239. The historic market town of Oakham with its shops and other attractions is only 4 miles to the east.

❸ Keep to a grassy path on your left, which goes round the field to the Lodge. At the Lodge you are on the historic county boundary between Leicestershire and Rutland. Hedge analysis shows it to be over 1,000 years old. At the Lodge keep ahead through the farm onto a grassy path. Go over a stile (the Lodge house is to your right).

❹ Now go straight on with a hedge on your right to the corner of Cold Overton Park Wood and through a gate on the right. Walk alongside the wood where you can see the ditch and bank comprising the pale of the former medieval deer park. It was here that Cold Overton Park and Flitteris Park had a common boundary. Markers show your way ahead, but at the third gate (wooden, no arrow) do not go through but turn right to follow the hedge to a stile at the far corner of the field.

❺ This brings you to a wide bridlepath. Turn right to follow it. It follows much of the eastern boundary of the former Flitteris deer park. It is well signposted and you see signs of the old boundary in a strip of the woodland you walk through. Beware boggy patches and overhanging trees. At last, in just less than 1 mile you reach the country lane between Braunston and Knossington.

❻ Turn right along the lane for just over 1 mile to reach your start. Watch for traffic. Note the interesting 'serpent' hedge at Lady Wood Farm on your right with Lady Wood behind. This woodland is a remnant of the great forest which existed here in medieval times. You will have noticed the many 'Lodges' hereabouts, which indicate this also.

WALK 5

RICHARD III AND BOSWORTH FIELD

Length: 6 miles

The Visitor Centre offers interest and refreshment

HOW TO GET THERE: From Market Bosworth follow 'Battlefield' signs down Shenton Lane (off the Market Street) for 1½ miles. Do not go to Shenton but turn sharp left at the canal bridge and follow the lane round to Shenton station ½ mile further on. You will pass a lane signposted 'Battlefield Centre' but do not take this.

PARKING: At the car park, Shenton station (toilets).

MAP: OS Landranger 140 Leicester & Coventry area (GR 398004).

Introduction

This fascinating walk includes a battle trail over Bosworth Field and visits the church at Sutton Cheney where, in 1485, Richard III prayed the night before he lost his crown in battle. It passes through the parkland south of Market Bosworth to reach that ancient market town with its fine buildings and superb floral displays. The Ashby Canal provides a link which is followed as it anachronistically converges on the battlefield. Narrow boats now ply back and forth only 100 yards away from the place where Richard fell. Battlefield, canal, church and famous market town comprise an unbeatable formula for the walker. Added to this is the beauty and charm of the west Leicestershire countryside, often missed by the busy tourist hurrying along the impersonal motorways which skirt the area.

History

Henry Tudor, marching from Milford Haven where he had made his landfall, approached the scene of the encounter, perhaps via the Roman road from Mancetter. Meanwhile Richard III, in residence in Nottingham, heard of the landing and took up position in Leicester. He then left the town and moved along the ridge to Sutton Cheney. Here he is reputed to have heard mass for the last time. Nearby, at the tumulus at the gated road to Market Bosworth, he is said to have addressed and rallied his troops before the battle. Richard then took up a strong position on Ambion Hill with marshland guarding his left flank. Though Henry Tudor was dismayed to see the glint of weapons from the King's considerable force of 12,000 men in a vantage point above him, he engaged the enemy fiercely with his mercenaries fighting bravely. However, the outcome might have been very different but for an incident which turned the tide in favour of Henry. The Earl of Stanley stood aside from the battle as a spectator with 6,000 men to the north, undecided which side to support. At the height of the battle, Henry rode with a body of men across to Lord Stanley's position, some say to persuade him to join the battle on Henry's side. Richard III, seeing this sudden move, thought that an attempt was being made to outflank him and charged down upon Henry with a company of his knights. A furious battle ensued and Lord Stanley decided to participate to such an extent that all was lost for the King. John Rous wrote: 'If I may speak truth to his honour, although small of body and weak in strength, he most valiantly defended himself as a noble knight to his last breath often exclaiming that he was betrayed.' This battle, described as the 'swan-song of chivalry', ended 30 years of family feud – the Wars of the Roses. This was the last time a King of England died fighting in battle, the

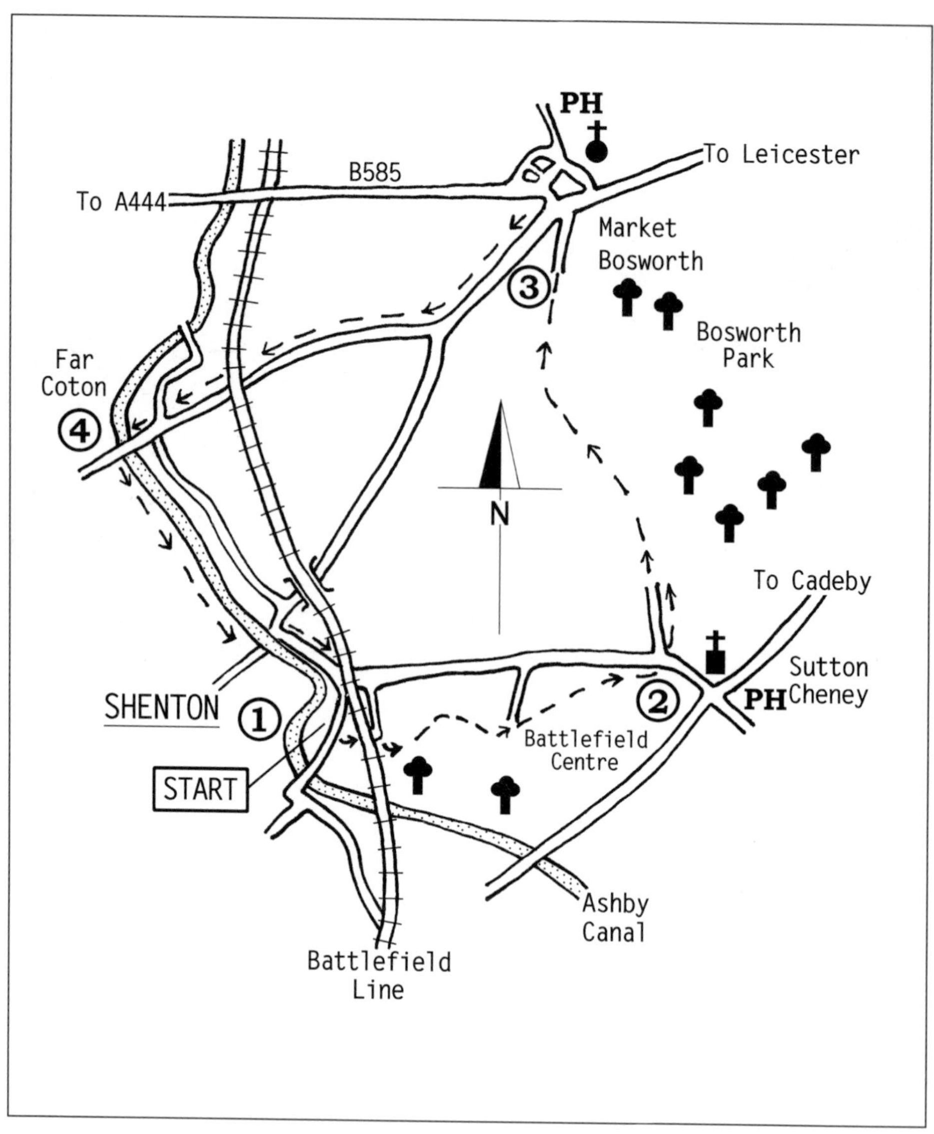

end of the Middle Ages and the beginning of a new dynasty destined to make Britain great in the world.

The Place

Would you like to re-live a great medieval battle and in the imagination,

The Battlefield Line runs from Shenton station to Shackerstone

recreate the charge of a body of knights in full armour with their king at their head? This is possible at Bosworth Field, where an award-winning recreation of the events of 22nd August 1485 has been successfully accomplished by means of trails, displays, films and models. Bosworth was a major turning point in English history, ranking with Hastings and the Battle of Britain.

HOSTELRY AND THIRSTQUENCHER

The Battlefield Centre and Buttery are open from 1st April to 31st October every day: Monday to Saturday 11 am to 5 pm, Sundays and bank holidays 11 am to 6 pm. During November and December opening hours are from 11 am to dusk on Sundays only, and in March from 11 am to 5 pm on Saturdays and Sundays. Telephone: 01455 290429. At Sutton Cheney the Hercules Inn and the Almshouse are beautifully situated behind the church. In Market Bosworth there are several inns and restaurants including the Dixie Arms, the Red Lion Hotel, the Forge and Bosworth Hall Hotel.

THE WALK

❶ Go over the railway and follow the path uphill, selecting 'Path 5 Battlefield Centre'. The route is easy to see and at the top of the hill on your right the royal standard of Richard III is often flying. This was the major area of the battle and information boards are well placed to give you the details. The path bears right and at the top of the hill if you look left you will see Sutton Cheney church in the distance. You will have had lovely views towards Market Bosworth as you came up the hill. As you reach the Battlefield Centre car park and picnic area turn left towards the centre for the cafe, shops, displays and exhibitions. To continue the walk, face the centre and then take the path to the left going over to wooden gates leading to a field. You can see Sutton Cheney church ahead. This is the walker's route. Do not turn into the main exit lane by mistake which is sharp left. You need to go straight ahead with the centre to your right. Follow this path for several fields until you reach a car park about ½ mile away. Here you find another map board of the trails.

❷ Go out onto the main road and turn right and continue into Sutton Cheney to look in the church and perhaps to take refreshment. Return the way you entered the village and just past the Almshouse turn right into the gated road to Market Bosworth. Remember to close all the gates along this pleasant lane which leads eventually, after 1¾ miles, into the parkland on the edge of Bosworth Country Park. A final gate takes you into the town.

❸ Go to the end of this lane and then turn left into Shenton Lane, which will take you out of town. Walk down this lane for ½ mile to a lane forking off right to Far Coton. Continue along this lane for 1 mile until you reach a canal bridge. You will have passed a sign to Far Coton a short distance back but you should ignore this and follow the 'Sibson 3' sign to the humped-back canal bridge.

❹ Once there, go down onto the towpath by crossing the bridge and turning left. Now follow this south for ¾ mile until you reach the aqueduct over the Shenton-Bosworth road. Fifteen yards beyond this aqueduct look for the steps, which will take you down to the road below. They are on your right. Down the steps and under the aqueduct next, turning right at the sign 'Bosworth Battlefield Centre'. Do not take the road to your left marked with the same sign but go on a little and on your right you will see the path into King

OTHER PLACES OF INTEREST

Nearby Bosworth Water Trust Leisure Centre and Water Park is open daily all year from 10 am to dusk. There is a charge per car. Telephone: 01455 291876. The Battlefield Line runs from Shenton station to Shackerstone. Telephone: 01827 880754.

Richard's Field. Go in here to examine the stone erected where he fell. This is also a pleasant place for a picnic and you can go up a slope to the canal to see narrow boats moored alongside here. Return to your car at Shenton station, which is just across the road turning right out of King Richard's Field.

King Richard III's memorial stone

WALK 6
LAUNDE ABBEY AND THE EARL OF ESSEX

Length: 3 miles

The remote grandeur of Launde Abbey

HOW TO GET THERE: From Oakham take the Tilton road. From the A47 take the B6047 turning off at Tilton on the Oakham road. From Uppingham take the A47, turn off at Belton and follow the signs.

PARKING: In Launde Abbey Park.

MAP: OS Landranger 141 Kettering & Corby (GR 798044).

INTRODUCTION

Launde Abbey is still relatively remote and surrounded by parkland – excellent for a picnic and space to run around. It was founded between 1119 and 1125 as the Augustinian Priory of St John the Baptist – a glade in the dense forest. It possessed lands and churches as far away as Nottinghamshire, Derbyshire, Northamptonshire, and Staffordshire as well as in Leicestershire and Rutland. The walk starts in Launde Park, with Launde Big Wood and

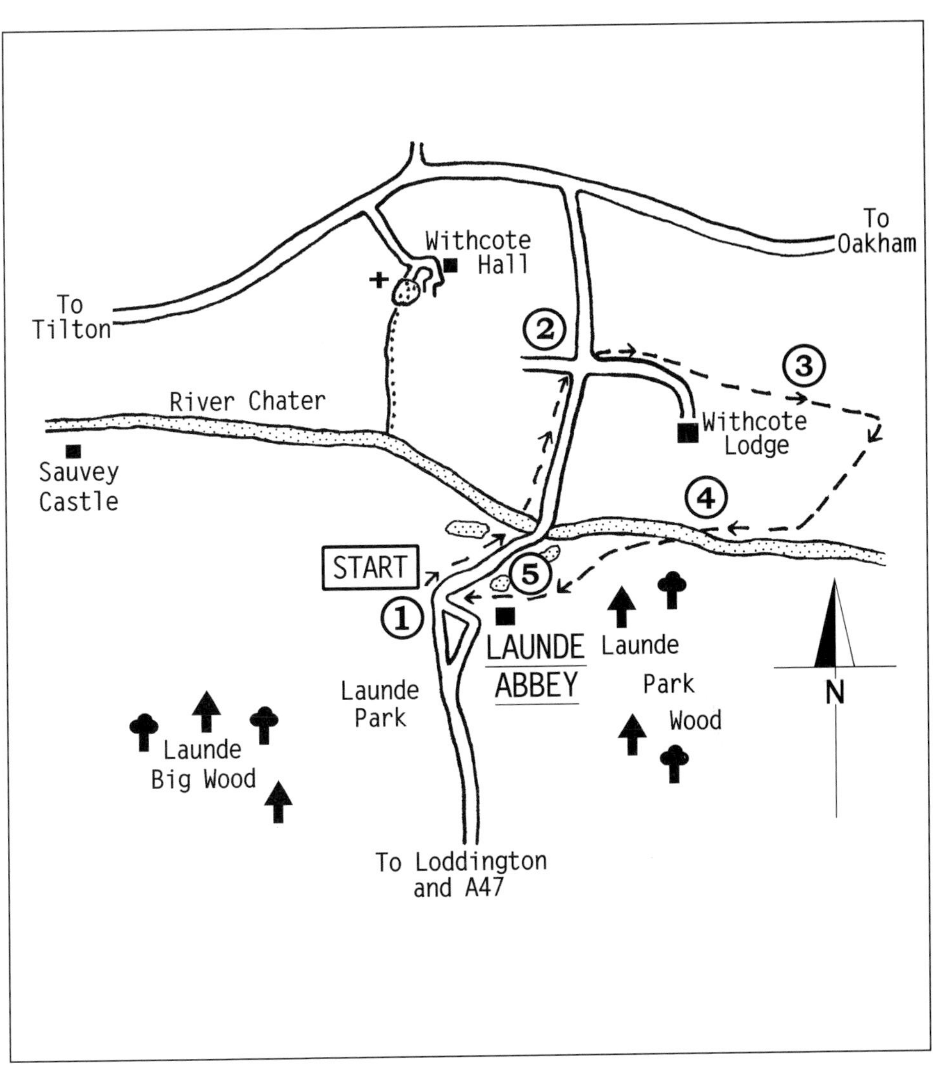

Launde Park Wood on either side. Hilly at first, the walk crosses the river Chater, then goes uphill and over fields towards Withcote Lodge, following the Leicestershire Round path back to Launde Abbey.

HISTORY

The man mainly responsible for the dissolution of the monasteries in England was Thomas Cromwell, Earl of Essex, 'the chief agent in bringing on the English reformation' and in making Henry VIII an absolute monarch. He had been interested in Launde since 1528 and wanted the property for himself. This was granted in 1540. Cromwell built a mansion at Launde, probably from the remains of the Priory. He also became Baron of Oakham. Since he was executed in 1540 he did not live to enjoy it. His son Gregory lived here until he died in 1551. In the chapel there is a memorial to him, 'one of the purest monuments of early Renaissance in England'. There stained glass is dated c.1450, but since later owners, William Holford (1611) and John Simpson (1763) 'modernised' the property it is hard to discover the original parts.

Launde Park

The Old Plough, Braunston, in the heart of Rutland

THE PLACE

As you will see on the walk, the canons altered the landscape, especially near the river Chater, where you can see diversions and dams. A little upstream is Sauvey Castle – 'the finest Norman motte-and-bailey in the county' (Pevsner). The Priory was dissolved in December 1539. Launde Abbey is now a Diocesan Retreat House and Conference Centre. It is often accessible but only open to the public on several occasions during the year. August Bank Holiday opening provides fun for all the family.

THE WALK

1 Start at the entrance gate to Launde Park. Go over the cattle grid and follow the lane down to the lakes. Carry on for about ½ mile to the sign for Braunston on the left, at the drive of Avenue Farm. If you wish to go left down the farm drive and then follow the

HOSTELRY AND THIRSTQUENCHER

The Old Plough, Braunston is only a few miles away – a traditional pub in the heart of Rutland, with Egon Ronay healthy eating options and appearing in the Good Beer Guide and Good Food Guide. Telephone: 01572 722714.

footpath to Withcote Hall you will have a fine view of the Hall, chapel and lake. There and back is a diversion of 1 mile in total. Return to the lane.

OTHER PLACES OF INTEREST

Hallaton Village Museum is situated in one of the most picturesque and historic villages in the county. Open May to October weekends 2.30 pm to 5 pm, also Bank Holiday Monday. Admission free. Telephone: 01858 555416.

❷ Otherwise, turn right between buildings on a wide track sign-posted to Braunston. At the bend do not go up to Withcote Lodge on the hill, but straight across the field (there are no markers here). Carry on through an open gate uphill at the right side of the field. At the corner go through a gate.

❸ Turn left to go round the edge of the field until you reach a bridle path sign at the head of a valley on the far side. Carry on a few yards, and then turn right to follow alongside the stream downhill to the left of the trees hiding the stream. At the next signpost carry straight on downhill on a wide grassy track, which curves round with the stream now on your left. Soon you cross the stream and the path leads to a gate.

❹ At the five-bar gate ignore the arrow and go round the field on the right-hand side, following a stream on your right. You reach a metal gate at the far side, where an arrow directs you across a pasture field diagonally left to a gate on the right of a hillock. Go through the gate and walk ahead uphill alongside the edge of trees to another five-bar gate.

❺ Launde Abbey is now behind the trees on your left. Go through the gate and carry on to the lane ahead. When you reach it turn left and walk back to your start.

WALK 7

THE NINE DAYS' QUEEN AT BRADGATE PARK

Length: 3½ miles

Old John Tower at Bradgate Park

HOW TO GET THERE: From Leicester take the B5327 to Anstey then to Newtown Linford. Go straight on and then bear right for the Hunt's Hill (Old John) car park.

PARKING: Hunt's Hill (Old John) car park. There are toilets here.

MAP: OS Landranger 129 Nottingham & Loughborough area (GR 522117).

INTRODUCTION

This walk, with wonderful views, takes you from Old John, nearly 700 feet above sea level, to the river Lin and the ruins of Bradgate House, birthplace of the ill-fated Lady Jane Grey. Skirting Cropston Reservoir and crossing into Swithland Woods, the return is again via Old John but following a different route. Bradgate Park was given to the people of Leicestershire by Charles Bennion in 1928. It was designated a country park in 1970 and extends over 850 acres. It is a magnet for tourists and visitors. In many ways, despite being only 7 miles from Leicester, it is a throwback to medieval times with heathland, bracken, woodland, grassland, craggy outcrops, ancient trees and herds of deer.

HISTORY

Bradgate was enclosed from the waste of Charnwood Forest to form a deer park, certainly before 1247. It was part of the Manor of Groby and owned by the Ferrers family. When Sir Edward de Grey was created Lord Ferrers in 1445 the estate passed into the line of this influential family; Sir John Grey married Elizabeth Woodville who, on his death, married Edward IV. It was this connection which gave Lady Jane Grey the right to the throne since she was a direct descendant of Henry VIII on her mother's side. Lady Jane Grey (1537–1554), the 'nine days' queen' of England was born at Bradgate. She was the grand-daughter of Henry VIII's sister, Mary. Her parents brought her up very strictly. She was gentle, quiet, clever and read books in several languages. She had no ambition to be queen but when she married Lord Guildford Dudley,

The ruins of Bradgate Park

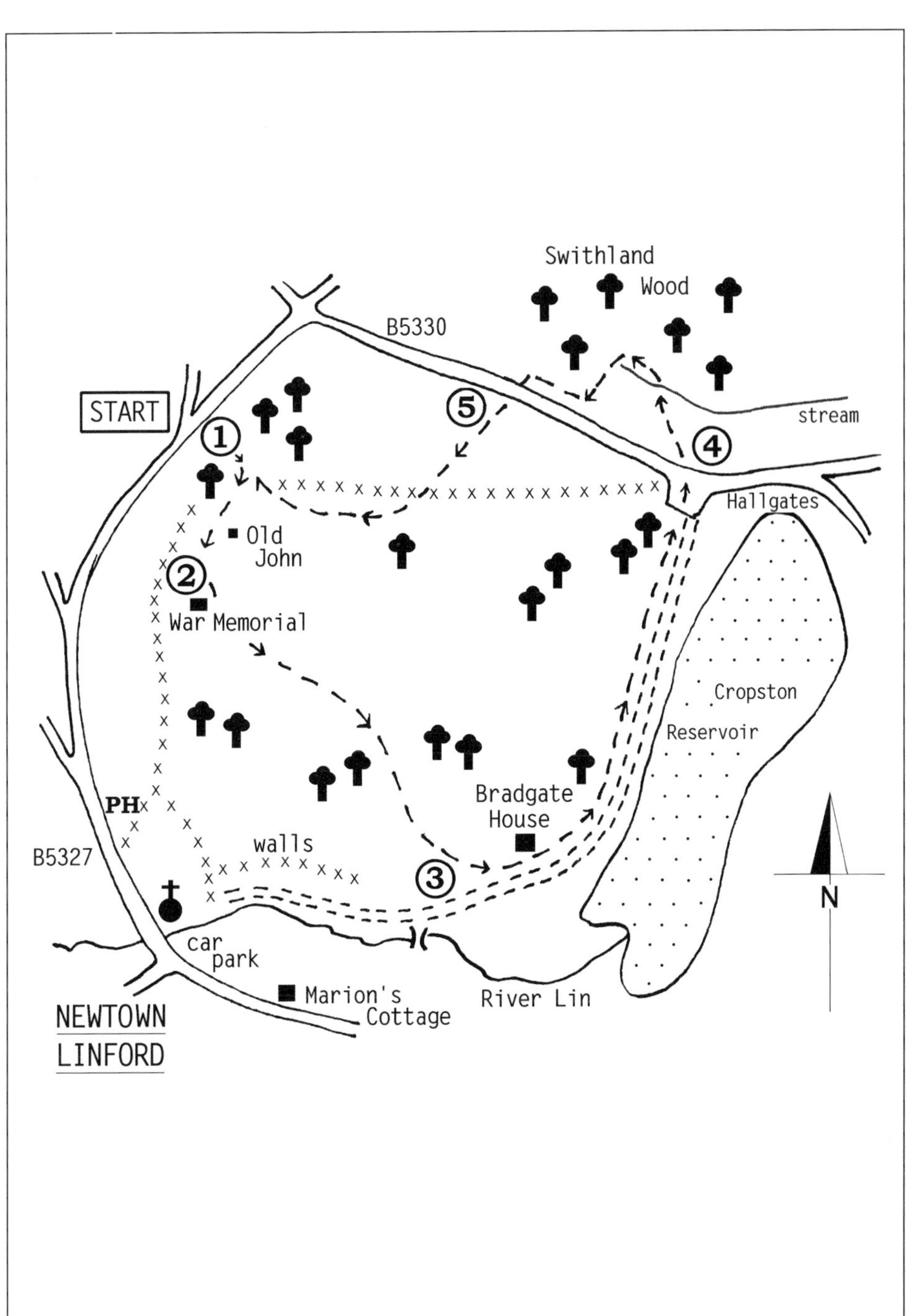

Swithland
Wood
B5330
START
1
5
4
stream
Hallgates
Old
John
2
War Memorial
Cropston
Reservoir
Bradgate
House
PH
walls
B5327
3
N
car
park
Marion's
Cottage
River Lin
NEWTOWN
LINFORD

son of the influential Duke of Northumberland, they used her to fulfil their design on the crown. The Duke persuaded the young King Edward VI to name Protestant Jane in his will as future queen rather than his Catholic half-sister Mary. On the death of the King in 1553, Northumberland proclaimed Jane queen on 10th July. However Henry VIII's daughter Mary arrived in London to great acclaim to be proclaimed queen on 19th July. Northumberland was too weak to oppose her and the consequence was that Lady Jane Grey and her husband were imprisoned and beheaded six months later in front of the Tower of London. It is said that all the oak trees at Bradgate were also beheaded (pollarded) in silent memory of Lady Jane. There is an exhibition in the house explaining this fascinating history.

THE PLACE

Bradgate House, now a ruin, was begun in 1490 and completed about 1510. It was one of the first unfortified brick built country houses in England. It may be that when the house was being constructed the villagers of Bradgate were removed outside the park, though it might have been earlier. They were removed to the 'new town at Linford' now known as Newtown Linford, outside the main gate. Bradgate Park Visitor Centre has displays about Lady Jane Grey. Open: April-October afternoons only (closed Mondays except Bank Holidays); November-March weekends only, 1pm to 4pm. Telephone: 0116 236 2713.

THE WALK

❶ From the car park go through the gap in the stone wall on to the woodland track. Two hundred yards ahead you pass through a wooden gate, just to the right of the toilets. You see Old John in front and the steep green slopes favoured by skiers in winter. Walk towards the war memorial which is the pillar to the right of the Old John Tower but as you get nearer bear left and make for Old John. Climb up to the toposcope for the best view and use it to name the distant features.

❷ Now go through the gap in the wall, which surrounds the nearby woodland and leads to the war memorial. A gap at the far side of the wood lets you through to the memorial. From here you can see to the west. Return through the wood and make your way downhill away from Old John. Aim for the red river cliff in the middle distance below. It does not matter really which path you take as long as you go downhill. You are going to reach the river Lin and the road alongside soon and then go left to the ruin of Bradgate

The War Memorial in Bradgate Park

House. Now you will see the red cliff better. It is a remnant of a desert wadi and has been scoured out by the river action plus man using the material for brick making. As you will notice, Bradgate House was one of the first unfortified brick-built country houses in the country, being started in 1490. Note also the Swithland Slate walls around.

HOSTELRY AND THIRSTQUENCHER

The Bradgate is situated in the Main Street, Newtown Linford. To the rear is a family garden play area and beer garden. Inside is a family lounge. There is an outstanding selection of traditional ales with Everards Old Original top of the list. There is a food bar and snack area with Chef's daily specials. Telephone: 01530 242239.

OTHER PLACES OF INTEREST

Kirby Muxloe Castle is a picturesque, ruined, fortified manor house dating from 1480 started by Lord Hastings, executed by order of Richard III before it was completed. Telephone: 01162 750555.

❸ Go along the road below the house following the river valley eastwards with Old John on your left on the skyline. You reach toilets on your right and now you walk alongside the Cropston Reservoir. In $^{3}/_{4}$ mile you come to the Hallgates car park with an information board.

❹ Exit the car park turning left at the main road B5330. Carry on for a short distance to Horseshoe Cottage Farm on your right. Immediately past the farm go over a stile with a footpath sign to Swithland. Cross over a pasture field diagonally to the far corner where you can cross a bridge and stile into Swithland Woods. Turn sharp left to follow a track along the stream until you reach a large bridge in 100 yards. Turn left to cross this bridge and follow the bridle road for 200 yards through woodland to a gate. Turn right into the car park located here and follow the track through the car park keeping fairly close to the wall on the left bordering the main road. Continue to the left of a litter bin and you soon come to a gap in the boundary wall. On the opposite side of the road you will see a sign showing the route to Old John.

❺ Cross the road carefully and proceed into the track with Old John clearly in view ahead of you. The wide track leads you to a kissing gate in the park wall. Once through this you can find your own route back to Old John and then return to your car by the same track as you approached via the gate in the wall and through the wood.

WALK 8
JEFFREY HUDSON'S OAKHAM

Length: 2 miles

The ancient Butter Cross in the market place at Oakham

HOW TO GET THERE: From Stamford and the A1 take the A606 to Oakham.

PARKING: There are several pay and display car parks in town.

MAPS: OS Explorer 15 Rutland Water & Stamford (GR 862088). Also Oakham Heritage Trail (map) from Tourist Information, Flores House, Oakham.

INTRODUCTION

An easy walk through the streets of historic Oakham, in the footsteps of Jeffrey Hudson, who was a 17th Court favourite and grew to be just three feet six inches tall. A fine Norman castle adds another dimension to this interesting stroll.

HISTORY

Jeffrey Hudson was born in 1619 in a small cottage next to Oakham's busy main street. He was baptised in nearby All Saints' church and probably attended the Old School in the churchyard which was built in 1584, only 35 years before his birth. His father was a butcher who would go to the Shambles in Market Place to sell his meat. He also kept and baited bulls for the Lord of the Manor, George Villiers, 1st Duke of Buckingham. The Butter Cross and

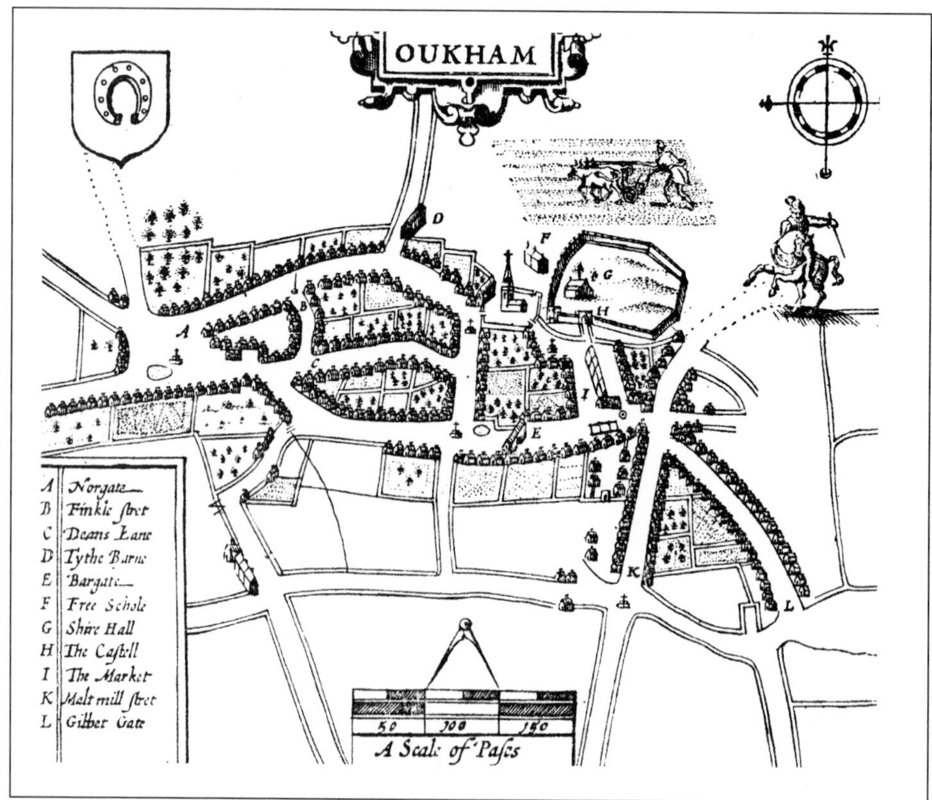

Town plan of Oakham, from John Speed's map of Rutland, 1611

The Old School built in 1584

Oakham Castle stand as reminders of this time and Jeffrey would have known them well. The gateway we see today was rebuilt by George Villiers who became Lord of the Manor in 1621 and it matches those at his mansion, Burley-on-the-Hill, one mile north of Oakham. It was here that nine-year-old Jeffrey, then only 18 inches tall, jumped out of a cold pie, in the presence of King Charles I and Queen Henrietta Maria. She was so taken by him that he became a court favourite for many years. In 1630 he was sent on the Queen's business to France but on his return he was captured by Flemish pirates. In 1637 he is reported fighting at the siege of Breda in Holland and was a Captain of the King's Horse in the English Civil War. In 1649, whilst in France, he fought a duel and killed the opponent who was foolish enough to turn up armed only with a water pistol. Later, Jeffrey was captured by Turkish pirates and enslaved for some years. At this time, he grew taller, eventually reaching three feet six inches in height. In 1679 he was implicated in the Popish Plot and imprisoned in the Gatehouse at Westminster. On his release he was awarded a pension from Charles II and died in 1682.

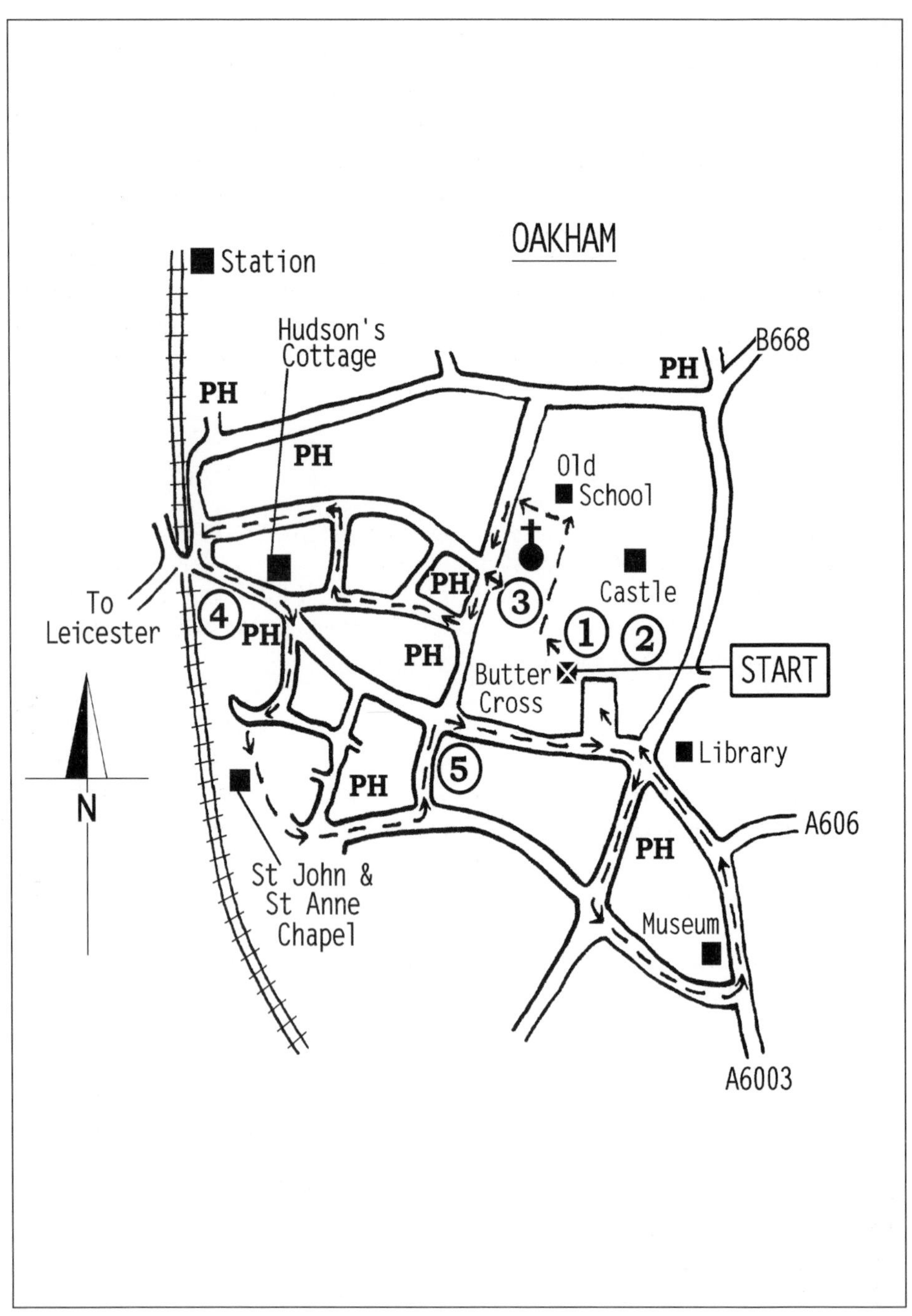
OAKHAM
Station
Hudson's Cottage
PH
PH
PH
B668
Old School
Castle
PH
3
1
2
To Leicester
4
PH
PH
Butter Cross
START
Library
5
PH
A606
PH
St John & St Anne Chapel
Museum
A6003
N

THE PLACE

Our walk includes the Butter Cross, market, castle, church, Old School and Jeffrey's former home (not open to the public). We walk the streets Jeffrey walked and see something of the Oakham Jeffrey would have seen. Surely Sir Jeffrey Hudson, as he became, exemplifies Rutland's motto Multum in Parvo – much in little. Oakham Castle is one of the finest examples of domestic Norman architecture in England, built between 1180 and 1190. Inside is a collection of over 200 horseshoes. Open: April to October 10 am to 1 pm, 2 pm to 5.30 pm (not Mondays); late October to late March closing at 4 pm. Sundays 2 pm to 5.30 pm. Admission free. The Rutland County Museum is open Monday to Saturday 10 am to 5 pm, Sunday 2 pm to 5 pm (4 pm late October to late March). Telephone: 01572 723654. Market days are Wednesday and Saturday.

THE WALK

❶ Start at the Butter Cross in the Market Place, opposite the post office. Cross over to the post office and then turn left down a short lane to Oakham Castle. Go through the horseshoe gate into the grounds. Walk round the grounds to your right following the line of the walls. Eventually you will return to your original position. Now you can go inside the castle.

❷ Leave the castle via Castle Lane. Turn right and go past the post office into Choir Close. All Saints' church will be in front of you. Turn right down a narrow footpath until you reach the Old School on your left. Pass through the gap on your left. Go past the Old School into Church Street. Turn left and walk along until you reach the gateway to All Saints' church on your left. Walk round to the south door of the church. Go inside to have a look around.

❸ From the south door walk directly to the other gate. The building in front of you is Oakham School chapel, close to other school buildings. Turn right along the footpath. At the end turn left and cross the road into Dean Street. Go along until you turn right at Finkey Street. Turn left as you reach Northgate. Walk along going round the corner on your left into Melton Road. Here you arrive at Jeffrey Hudson's cottage.

HOSTELRY AND THIRSTQUENCHER

There are many cafes, restaurants, pubs and take-aways in Oakham – some call it 'the gourmet capital of the East Midlands.' For novelty try the Colonel's Cafe in Rutland County Museum.

❹ Cross the road into Westgate.

Walk round into St Anne's Close. Peer through the gateway of St John & Anne's Hospital to see the old chapel. Now go down William Dalby Walk into South Street. Then past the Friends Meeting House into Goal Street. You are now back onto the High Street.

OTHER PLACES OF INTEREST

Rutland Farm Park, Uppingham Road, Oakham is a Victorian farmyard with rare breeds. Telephone: 01572 756789. The Anglian Birdwatching Centre, Egleton, has a viewing gallery overlooking three lagoons where water birds gather all year. Telephone: 01572 770651. All the attractions of Rutland Water are only a few miles away.

❺ Turn right into the High Street. You pass the Market Place on your left. In a short distance turn right into Mill Street, then left into South Street, finally turning left again into Catmose Street, past Rutland County Museum, to return to your start.

WALK 9
THE METEOROLOGICAL SQUIRE OF LYNDON HALL

Length: 4 miles

Lyndon Hall

HOW TO GET THERE: From the A1 at Stamford take the A606 to Oakham but before Empingham bear left for Rutland Water South Shore. From the A6003 turn off for Manton and Lyndon.

PARKING: Sensible parking near the church in Lyndon.

MAP: OS Explorer 15 Rutland Water & Stamford (GR 908044).

INTRODUCTION

Lyndon Hall sits imposingly like a French chateau on the higher slopes of the Chater valley. Nearby the clock tower, gateways and gardens of the Hall with the much-restored church of St Martin, complete one of Rutland's finest picture-postcard scenes. The Hall was completed in 1677 and not so long after, in 1722, it was the birthplace of Thomas Barker, now recognised as one of England's most important meteorologists – some say 'the Father of English Meteorology'. From here it is an easy walk to the start of Rutland Water, with a return along quiet roads and paths.

HISTORY

Thomas was the son of Samuel Barker (1686–1759), noted scholar of Hebrew. Sarah, his mother, was the daughter of William Whiston (1667–1752), famous divine, philosopher and mathematician, who is buried at Lyndon. So Thomas had an excellent pedigree for scholarship and observation. It was in the Hall that Thomas began his weather journals in 1733 and maintained them for over 60 years. Besides invaluable weather records he commented on natural phenomena, crops and garden plants. He notes a tornado: 'I saw it pass from Pilton over Lyndon Lordship, like a black smoky cloud, with bright Breaks; an odd whirling motion and a roaring noise like a distant wind'. Thomas also made astronomical observations. He wrote theological works and we can imagine him regularly worshipping in the nearby church, even preaching there. The world-famous author of *The Natural History of Selborne,* Gilbert White (1720–1793) was his brother-in-law. They often visited each other and it is believed that Thomas encouraged Gilbert to start his records.

So, in this tiny, unremarkable Rutland village we find an observant and unique country squire whose weather records, kept quietly over 60 years are being used by present day weathermen, to recreate weather patterns in England during the past 250 years. Thomas died on 29th December 1809, almost 88 years of age. His closeness to nature is emphasised by the fact that he lived all that time as a vegetarian. How he would have enjoyed recording weather changes in Lyndon induced by Rutland Water! Perhaps his ghost still lingers in the garden around the Hall longing to do so.

THE PLACE

Our walk starts at the church where you can search for the headstones of the Barker family, which mainly stand at the west wall of the churchyard. You can glimpse the Hall (not open to the public) through the archway. In the church there is a booklet about Thomas Barker and Lyndon village. Opposite

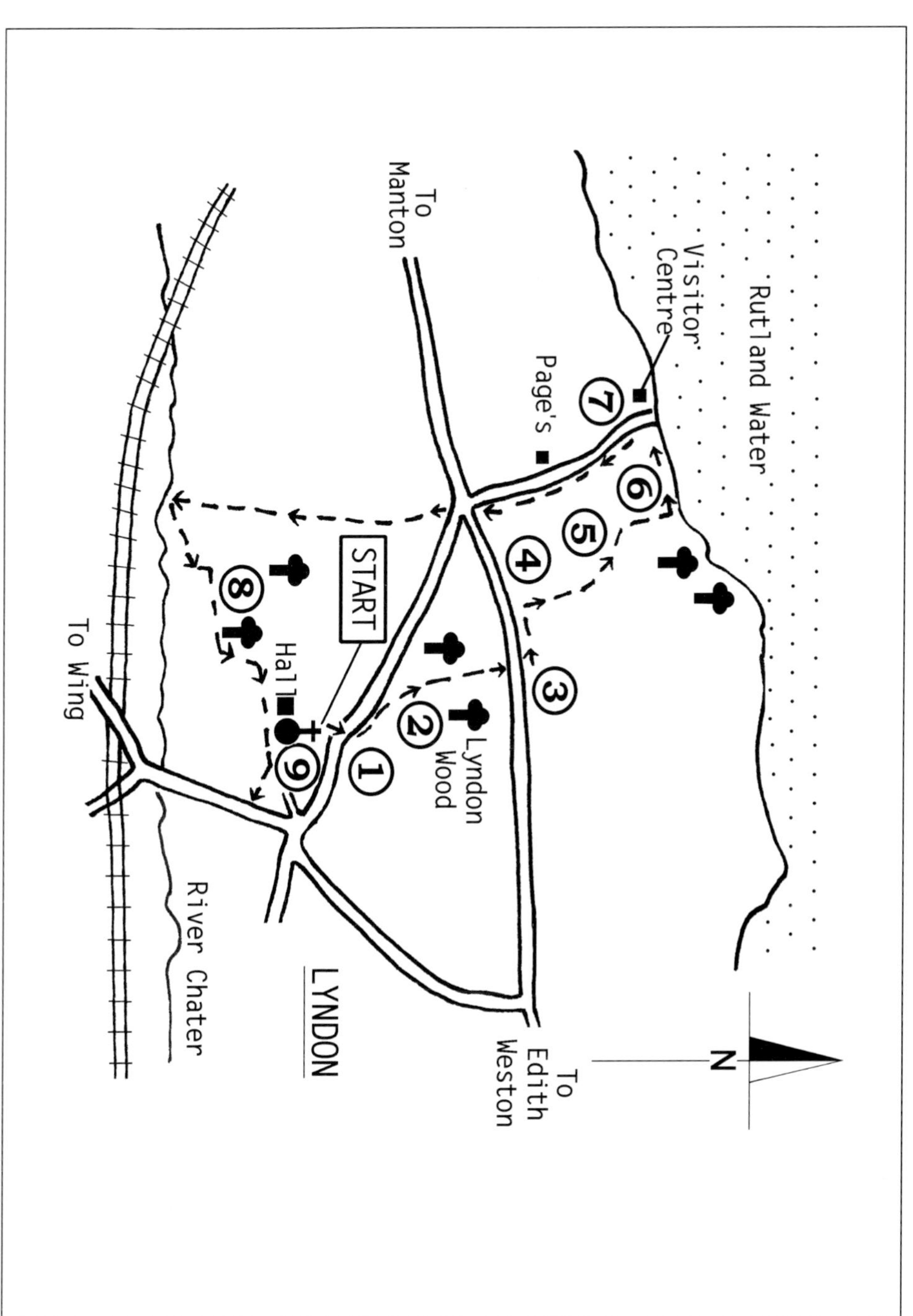

Rutland Water
Visitor Centre
Page's
To Manton
START
Hall
Lyndon Wood
To Wing
River Chater
LYNDON
To Edith Weston
N
1
2
3
4
5
6
7
8
9

you will see Lyndon Top Hall, built about the same time as Lyndon Hall, but superior in style. Both Halls were built by Abel and Thomas Barker of Hambleton, distant cousins of Samuel Barker. Further along the walk, near Rutland Water, you will see on the north shore Hambleton Hall, once an ancestral home of the Barker family. Now Rutland Water has separated their lands. As you come to the Lyndon Nature Reserve and Visitor Centre the displays will remind you of the natural interests of Thomas Barker.

THE WALK

❶ Start at the church. As you come out of the drive turn left onto the road. Walk along this avenue of trees to the bridlepath sign on the right and go through the wooden five-bar gate.

❷ Walk diagonally towards Lyndon Wood where you will see a five-bar gate. Go through and into the path alongside a new plantation. Carry on the wide track to the main road.

❸ Turn left and walk along the road to the bridlepath sign about 200 yards on the right.

❹ Turn right to walk along the hedge-side to your left. Go on to the corner of the field, through some rough ground, and then bear left to a gate marked 'Lakeland Estates'. Go through to the next gate and beyond.

❺ Now follow the path downhill with Rutland Water in front. Go to double wooden gates at the bottom of the hill to join the perimeter path round the reservoir.

❻ Turn left along the wide stoney path until you reach Lyndon Nature Reserve Visitor Centre with its car park.

❼ From the Visitor Centre, go up the lane to the main road, calling in at Page's Tea Room. Cross to the opposite side onto a wide farm track (sign). Walk alongside trees on your left. At a white stoney track turn left to follow it alongside a wood into a

HOSTELRY AND THIRSTQUENCHER

Page's Tea Room, Lyndon Road, Manton, offers breakfast, lunches and cream teas. Mediterranean courtyard with panoramic views of Rutland Water. Telephone: 01572 737371.

St Martin's church, Lyndon

field with a hedge to your right. Bear left as the path goes round the corner. At a marker post turn right along a field path. At the next marker post in the far corner turn left round the field.

❽ Turn right at the next marker post to go through a wood. Once through, turn left and follow round the outside of the wood, then south of Thomas Barker's Lyndon Hall. Follow the path round to the village lane.

OTHER PLACES OF INTEREST

Lyndon Hill Visitor Centre & Nature Reserve, south shore, Rutland Water. Telephone: 01572 737378. Normanton Church Museum, south shore Rutland Water tells the story of the construction of Rutland Water. Telephone: 01572 653026/7. Rutland Water Garden Nursery Ltd., Lyndon Road, Manton. Telephone: 01572 737711. Rutland Water Cycling, Normanton car park. Telephone: 01780 460705. Rutland Water Golf Course, licensed tea room and garden, Lodge Farm, Manton Road. Telephone: 01572 737525. Wing Maze, near Wing village, is a rare turf maze, one of the few in the country. Why not walk its path as it is believed monks did whilst making their penance?

❾ Here, turn left and at Post Office Lane turn left again to go to the end of the lane. Look to your right and you see an impressive portico with blue gates. Go through and follow the path round to another gate, which brings you out to the church and your start. Please close the gates. You have a good view of Lyndon Hall from this secret pathway.

WALK 10
THE MURDEROUS EARL OF FERRERS – STAUNTON HAROLD HALL

Length: $2^1/_2$ miles

Staunton Harold Hall and church

HOW TO GET THERE: Ashby de la Zouch can be reached via the A42 or the A511. From here take the B587 for Staunton Harold which is 3 miles to the north.

PARKING: At Staunton Harold Hall.

MAP: OS Landranger 128 Derby & Burton-on-Trent (GR 378209).

INTRODUCTION

This must be one of England's most outstanding walks. On old estate roads, it offers the idyllic scene of Staunton Harold Hall, church and lakes, described by Nicholas Pevsner as 'unsurpassed in the country, certainly as far as Englishness is concerned'. Now the Hall is a Sue Ryder Home and the nearby church is National Trust property. Who could guess that the last peer of the realm to be hanged was Lord of the Manor here?

HISTORY

Laurence Shirley, 4th Earl of Ferrers (1720–1760) had a faithful family retainer, John Johnson, who acted as the Earl's steward. At first both got on very well together. However, there was a dispute when Johnson administered a trust for the Earl's former wife to the dissatisfaction of the Earl. The Earl tried to sack Johnson and terminate his tenancy on the estate, but this seemed slow to work. Therefore on 13th January 1760 the Earl invited Johnson to the hall. After one hour the Earl was heard to cry out, 'Down on your knees, your time has come, you must die!' Then there was a shot. A servant, called to the room, saw Johnson alive but covered in blood. The well-known Dr Kirkland from Ashby de la Zouch was called but he could do nothing and the next morning Johnson died. The Earl was arrested and kept in custody at Ashby, then Leicester gaol and finally London, where he awaited trial by his peers at Westminster. Pleading not guilty due to occasional insanity failed and he was sentenced to hang at Tyburn. He had asked to be beheaded in the Tower but this had been refused. Dr Kirkland was chief witness for the prosecution and the offending bullet plus the silken hangman's rope used to hang the Earl, found their way into the doctor's famous museum in Ashby. The Earl died in style, travelling to his execution in his landau wearing his richly embroidered wedding suit. He was allowed the privilege of a silken cord instead of a rope and became not only the first person to die on the 'new drop' but the last peer of the realm to be hanged. His body was taken to Surgeon's Hall for dissection and then buried in St Pancras church. Tradition avers that his remains were disinterred and brought back to Staunton Harold. John Johnson is buried in the churchyard at Breedon-on-the-Hill, Leicestershire, where a large upright stone marks his grave.

THE PLACE

Staunton Harold Hall lacks a village since this was removed in favour of sheep ranching in the 14th century. The Shirley family held the Manor for over five centuries. The present hall was designed and built by Washington,

The Golden Gates leading to the Hall

5th Earl. The formal gardens of the late 17th century were mostly swept away by the same earl who replaced them with more natural scenery. Escaping demolition in the 1950s, the hall was sold in 1954. It is now a Sue Ryder Specialist Palliative Care Home and only the coffee shop, which is part of the Hall, is open to the public. Holy Trinity church is one of the few built during the Commonwealth. It was begun in 1653 by Sir Robert Shirley, an ardent Royalist, as an act of piety and defiance 'when all things sacred were

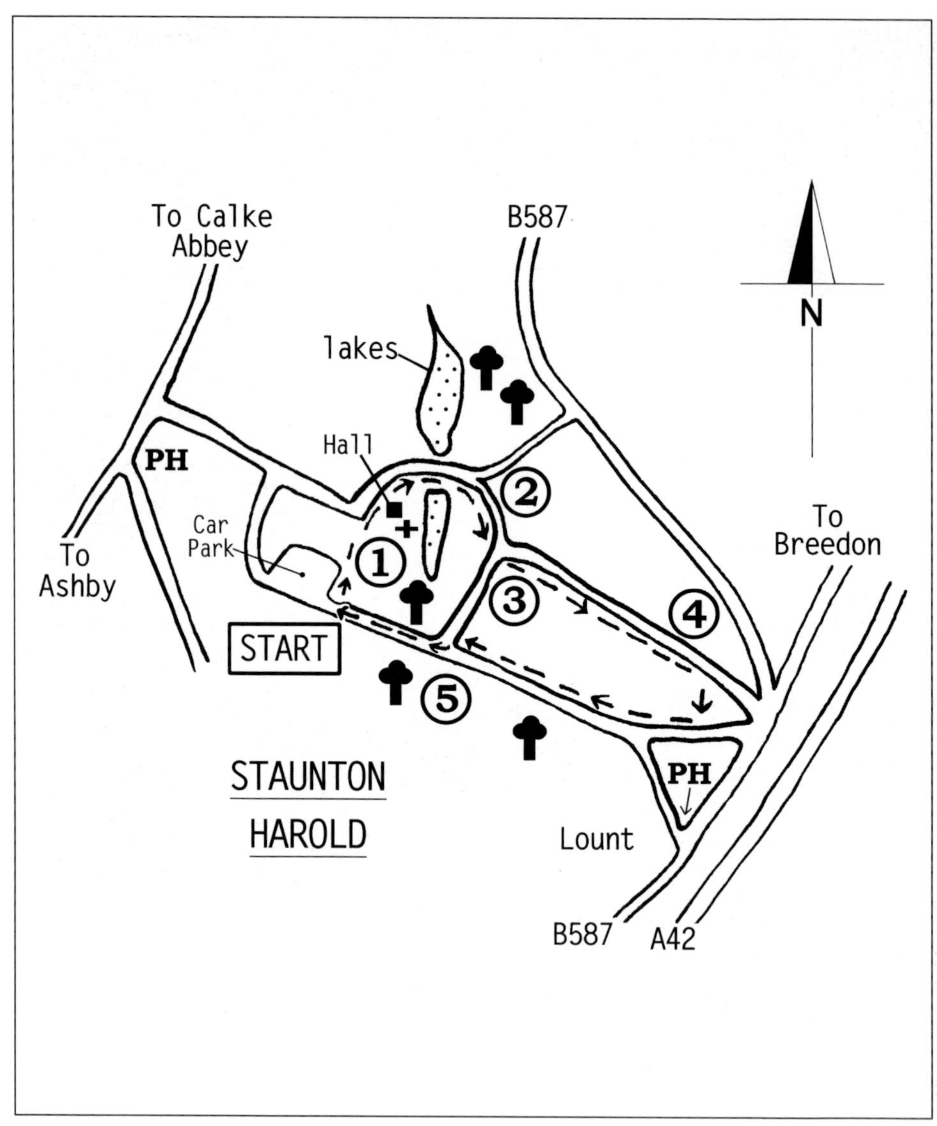

throughout the Nation either demolisht or profaned.' Completed in 1665 it retains the original cushions, hangings, panelling and painted ceiling, also a wrought iron screen by Robert Bakewell. Open: March to the end of October, Wednesday to Sunday and Bank Holiday Mondays 11 am to 1 pm; 2 pm to 5 pm.

Metal sculpture outside the Staunton Stables Tea Room

THE WALK

❶ Start in the car park. Go to the north-east corner, cross the footbridge and follow the Yew Walk which brings you to a driveway behind the Hall. Continue to walk along this driveway as it runs between two lakes to the Golden Gates, which have barley sugar shaped columns and the talbot and the stag as supporters.

❷ Once through the gates, turn right along the tarmac Coach Road. Here, on your right, you will see one of the best views in England. Go on to the cattle grid, which leads you into the approach lane to the Hall (you probably came in by this entry).

HOSTELRY AND THIRSTQUENCHER

Staunton Harold Hall Coffee Shop and the Staunton Stables Tea Room are open Tuesday to Sunday, 11 am to 5 pm (4.30 pm in winter). The Nursery Tea Room is available on Mondays and at other times.

OTHER PLACES OF INTEREST

You can walk to Calke Abbey (National Trust), only 1 mile north of Staunton Harold. Sir Vauncey Harpur Crewe kept Calke Abbey house untouched so that it remains as it was in the 1880s. It is open from the end of March to the end of October, Saturdays to Wednesdays inclusive, 11 am to 5 pm.

❸ Go ahead into the lane and walk for about ½ mile until you reach the thatched Coach Road Cottage, on your right. Take care along the road, as some cars will come this way.

❹ Just before the Cottage, cross the stile on your right. Bear left round the Cottage keeping close to the building and make for a metal gate, which opens onto the Old Coal Road – once the route for coal from Lount Pit to the Hall. Turn right uphill next to a spinney then as the track forks, you keep straight on.

❺ In about ½ mile you come to a tarmacked lane at a bend. Go through an open gateway, then ahead over a small bridge. The church and hall are beyond the Wilderness Woodland on your right. Keep on to return to the car park

WALK 11

THOMAS TELFORD AND FOXTON LOCKS

Length: 5 miles

View under Rainbow Bridge, Foxton Locks

HOW TO GET THERE: From Market Harborough take the A4304 and turn off at Lubenham or take the B6047 out of town to the north and you see the left turn to Foxton in about 2 miles.

PARKING: There is an excellent car park next to the village hall in Middle Street, Foxton.

MAP: OS Landranger 141 Kettering, Corby & surrounding area (GR 701899).

INTRODUCTION

The canal revolution has left a wonderful legacy for walkers in Leicestershire. Following the canal network gives a quiet serenity away from the bustle of busy roads. Moreover, there are spectacular remains to be seen: beautiful brick bridges, aqueducts, cottages, inns, locks, inclined planes, reservoirs and canal feeders, tunnels, wharves and tramways. Added to this are the lovely narrow boats, which give so much colour and life to the waterways today. Foxton Locks is one of the outstanding sights in Britain. It comprises a staircase of ten locks, which lift the canal 75 feet and enable the Grand Union Canal to complete the last link 'in the great line of canals, which extend from the Thames to the Humber'.

HISTORY

The locks were constructed on the advice of the engineer James Barnes and built between 1808 and 1814. They are a miracle of early 19th century engineering. They are joined at the Bottom Lock by a branch canal from Market Harborough opened in 1809. When the link was finally made into Northamptonshire and the Grand Junction Canal at Long Buckby, a daily service could be offered to 'all parts of England'. However, Foxton Locks might never have existed if the great engineer Thomas Telford had had his way. Called in to advise the canal company in 1803, he suggested that the route should not cross the high ground but go along the present course of the Harborough branch, then south across the Welland Valley eventually joining the Grand Junction Canal at Long Buckby. The Harborough branch was built, and we follow it along our walk, but, in 1809, Telford's advice to carry on south was ignored and the decision was taken to build Foxton Locks and go south from that point to Long Buckby. It remains important that the great Scottish engineer, Telford (1757–1834) who built the Caledonian Canal, the Gotha Canal in Sweden and the magnificent suspension bridges over the Menai Straits and at Conway, was associated with canal building in Leicestershire. He was the most influential engineer of his time who 'built more bridges in Great Britain than anyone before or since' and his imprint is still seen on the landscape today.

THE PLACE

Recent and continuing restoration and conservation work has made the entire lock system a very fine sight and the inclined plane has also been cleared so that the visitor can inspect it closely. The former engine house is now a museum. One of the most rewarding aspects is to look for the small

One of the locks at Foxton built between 1808 and 1814

details such as signs, nameplates, old machinery and the art forms associated with the great canal era. The narrow boats themselves provide intriguing details and a never-ending variety of names such as *Pocahontas, Ruddy Duck, Silver Shadow, Admiral.* Foxton Inclined Plane Canal Museum is open summer 10am to 5pm daily; winter 11am to 4pm (not Monday & Tuesday). Telephone: 0116 2792657.

THE WALK

❶ Start at the car park next to the village hall in Middle Street. Turn left and walk down to Woodgate where you find the canal and Foxton Field Centre. At the canal, turn left to follow the towpath. Walk along this quiet and pleasant path for 3 miles as the canal turns south to Market Harborough. You will pass several bridges.

❷ Go under Uncle Tom's Bridge No 12 which is where the B6047 road crosses and continue along the towpath to the next bridge where you ascend, cross and then go down to the towpath which is now on the opposite side of the canal. Carry on for about 300 yards until you come to a narrow iron footbridge.

❸ Turn right to cross a stile here, go down the bank and turn right towards a marker post at a row of trees. Then go alongside the trees and the edge of the field to the next marker post ahead. Just beyond is a signpost. Take the Foxton direction alongside the field. Bear right across a former shooting range to the marker post ahead. You follow a drive for some distance then at the next marker post turn left to walk alongside a fence/hedge at the side of the field in the direction of Gartree Prison ahead. At the end of the fence go over to the next marker post ahead, then over a stile into a lane at the side of the prison. In autumn the field here will be ploughed and may be troublesome to cross. In summer there should be a path through the crop.

❹ Turn right along the lane at the side of the prison wall. At the main road turn right for 20 yards to the footpath sign. Cross over the stile into the field, which at the time of

HOSTELRY AND THIRSTQUENCHER

There is a shop at Bottom Lock, also the Bridge 61 pub, which has all the atmosphere redolent of the canal era inside. There are snack and basket meals, also main courses with an all day menu, children's menu and specials board. This freehouse has Everards Old Original alongside Beacon and Tiger, Adnams Bitter etc. Telephone: 0116 2792285. The excellent Black Horse pub is also en route. Telephone: 01858 545250.

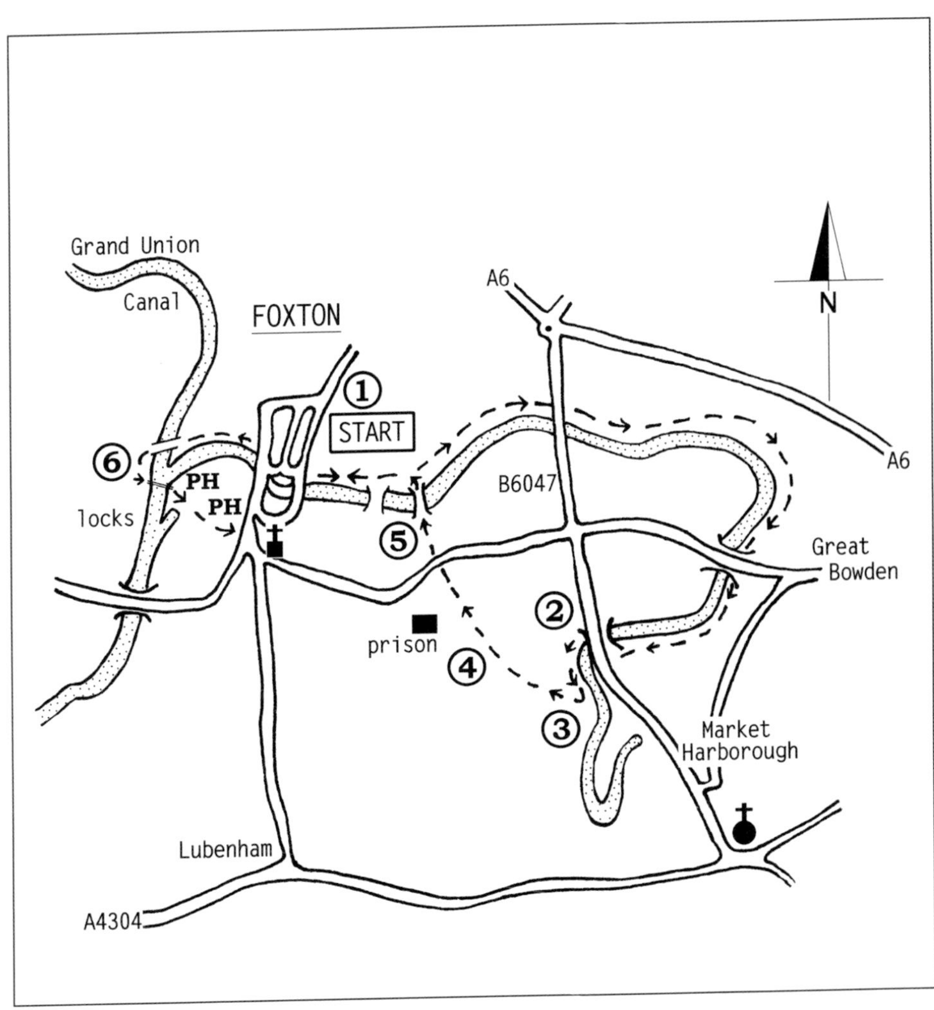

walking was a bean field with a good pathway through the middle leading down to the canal.

❺ Cross over the footbridge, turn left along the towpath and return to the swingbridge, near where you began. If you wish to end the walk here turn right at Foxton Field

OTHER PLACES OF INTEREST

Market Harborough is a pleasant historic town with St Dionysius' church, the 17th century timber-framed Old Grammar School and the Harborough Museum, Adam & Eve Street, open Monday to Saturday, 10 am to 4.30pm; Sunday 2 pm to 5 pm. Telephone: 01858 821085. Market days Tuesdays, Fridays and Saturdays.

Centre and go back to the car park. You can go on to Foxton Locks by car. However, if you have the energy to walk another mile, go along the towpath to Foxton Locks Basin (you can divert to the Black Horse nearby if you wish for a while).

❻ At the Basin, cross Rainbow Bridge No 62, then walk across Bottom Lock to the shop and Bridge 61 pub. Carry on along the rough road for ½ mile when you come to the main road. Turn left downhill past St Andrew's church on your right and the Black Horse on your left. Go over the bridge and turn right to return to the car park.

WALK 12
THE EARL OF MOIRA: GEORGIAN INDUSTRIALIST

Length: $2\frac{1}{2}$ miles

The entrance to Moira Furnace

HOW TO GET THERE: From Leicester take the A50/A511 to Ashby de la Zouch, then the B5003 to Moira and the National Forest Visitor Centre on Bath Lane.

PARKING: In the car park of the National Forest Visitor Centre (free).

MAP: OS Landranger 128 Derby & Burton-upon-Trent (GR 305156).

INTRODUCTION

North-west Leicestershire is very different from the rest of the county. For at least 200 years it had been the centre of industry including coal mines, canals, tramways, brick-making, steam engines, blast furnaces, railways and the like. Its landscape was scarred and disfigured by industry in an era when there was little concern for the environment. However, over the years this industry has changed and declined so that the last active collieries in the area closed some years ago. It is helpful to visit the Snibston Discovery Park at Coalville to get some idea of the impact of mining on the district. There is a fascination with this industrial landscape and its relics but amidst it all there are still farms, green fields, lovely walks and beauty as well as the odd architectural gem. This walk will show you the Leicestershire nobody knows – or at least, very few. For it is not yet a tourist area, although attempts are being made to capitalise on the industrial landscape and now the M42 crosses the area more people will stop over in future. The walk starts at the National Forest Visitor Centre, which is full of attractions and described as 'England's most ambitious environmental project of the new millennium'. You then follow the Ashby Woulds Heritage Trail to Moira and return via Sarah's Wood.

HISTORY

The Moira Furnace was built about 1804 by the Earl of Moira who wanted to exploit the mineral wealth of the Ashby Woulds, close by. After the area was enclosed in 1800 the way was open for the Earl, who owned the land, to mine the coal reserves which were then used to smelt local ironstone. The Ashby Canal, next to the Moira Furnace, brought coal, ironstone and limestone from the Ashby Woulds and elsewhere. However, the furnace and foundry were under-used and largely restricted to serving the local market. The Coal Measure ironstone was poor quality and the coal too valuable to waste as coking coal for smelting, thus, by about 1812 it ceased operations. Nevertheless, due to the work of the Leicestershire Industrial History Society in restoration, the Moira Furnace is a scheduled ancient monument and a rare example.

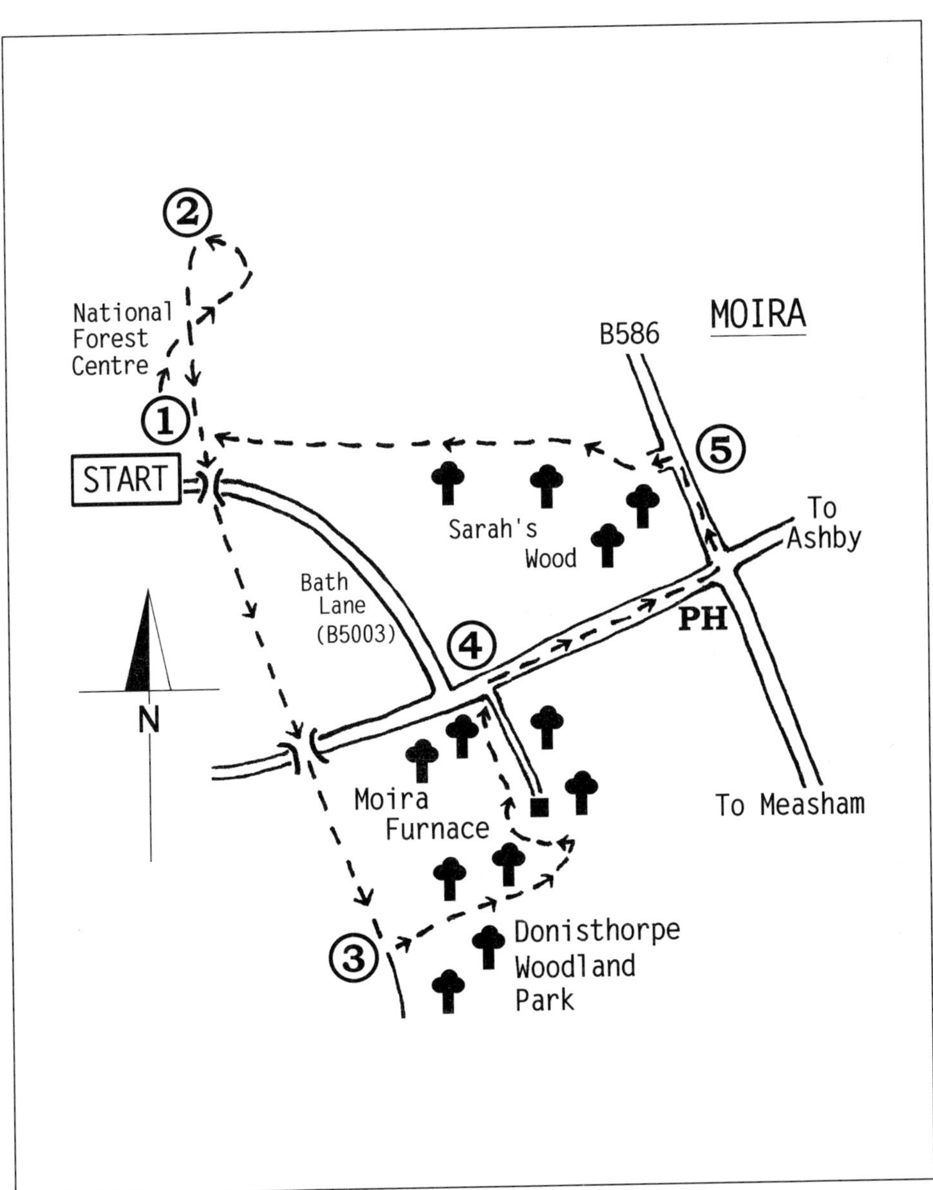

THE PLACE

You can walk around the industrial graveyard between Moira, Donisthorpe and Oakthorpe partly along the disused railway and canal to discover the

The Moira Furnace is a scheduled ancient monument

remnants of a once great and widespread industry. You can stand in front of the blast furnace at Moira, follow the canal, see former wharves, pass by miners' cottages, walk over the old spoil heaps of the collieries and stroll beside the 'flashes', lakes formed by the subsidence of the land due to underground mining. You can see attempts being made to turn the dereliction into a restored landscape and the New National Forest is one hope for the future. Opening times: National Forest Centre daily 10 am to

6 pm (summer); 10 am to 4.30 pm (winter). Telephone: 01283 216633. Moira Furnace and Museum open Wednesday to Sunday 12 noon to 4 pm; site/park from dawn to dusk. Telephone: 01283 224667.

THE WALK

❶ Start at the car park of the National Forest Visitor Centre. Join the Ashby Woulds Heritage Trail by going to the right of the children's play area, then follow the sign on the left (in front of an old railway bridge) and the path which goes under another old bridge then bears left round the field. At the next sign go left to join the old railway, once the Ashby and Nuneaton Joint Railway operating between 1873 and 1931. The Trail now follows this.

❷ You are now on the line of the old railway, which you follow for about 1 mile. There are information boards along the Trail and since this section is on a high embankment you will have had a good view around.

❸ When you reach the sign 'Donisthorpe Colliery' do not go into this newly-created Woodland Park but turn left down to a lane. Go ahead onto a narrow path in the trees. Carry on, ignore paths and signs to the right and left. You arrive at a tarmac path and the Lime Kilns. Carry on until soon you reach a restored section of the Ashby Canal. Bear left to the Moira Furnace and Museum nearby. There is a tea room, toilets and a craft workshop on the site. Now is the time to follow local paths to explore the site.

❹ When you are ready, go down the exit road to the main road. Turn right and walk to the cross-roads (the Woodman pub is on the corner). Turn left onto the B586 and look for Sarah's Wood on your left, in about 200 yards.

❺ Turn left into Sarah's Wood (which closes at 7 pm). Go towards the toilets then follow the tarmac path which leads to the National

HOSTELRY AND THIRSTQUENCHER

There is a restaurant and snack bar at the National Forest Visitor Centre and a tea room at the Moira Furnace. The Woodman pub is en route. Telephone: 01283 218316.

OTHER PLACES OF INTEREST

Donington le Heath Manor House, near Coalville, dates from 1280, one of the few domestic 13th century buildings remaining intact in the country. Open daily Easter to end September 11 am to 5 pm, October to March 11 am to 3 pm. Telephone: 01530 817214 (tea room).

The National Forest Visitor Centre, Moira

Forest Visitor Centre car park a short distance on the far side. Sarah's Wood is an example of 25 acres of farmland being turned over to a varied woodland with a play area, accessibility for wheelchairs and information boards.

WALK 13

A HERO OF WATERLOO AT GADDESBY

Length: $4\frac{1}{2}$ miles

The monument in St Luke's church commemorates the Hero of Waterloo

HOW TO GET THERE: Follow the A607 from either Leicester or Melton Mowbray turning off for Gaddesby onto the B674 at Rearsby.

PARKING: Sensible parking in the village.

MAP: OS Landranger 129 Nottingham & Loughborough area (GR 688129).

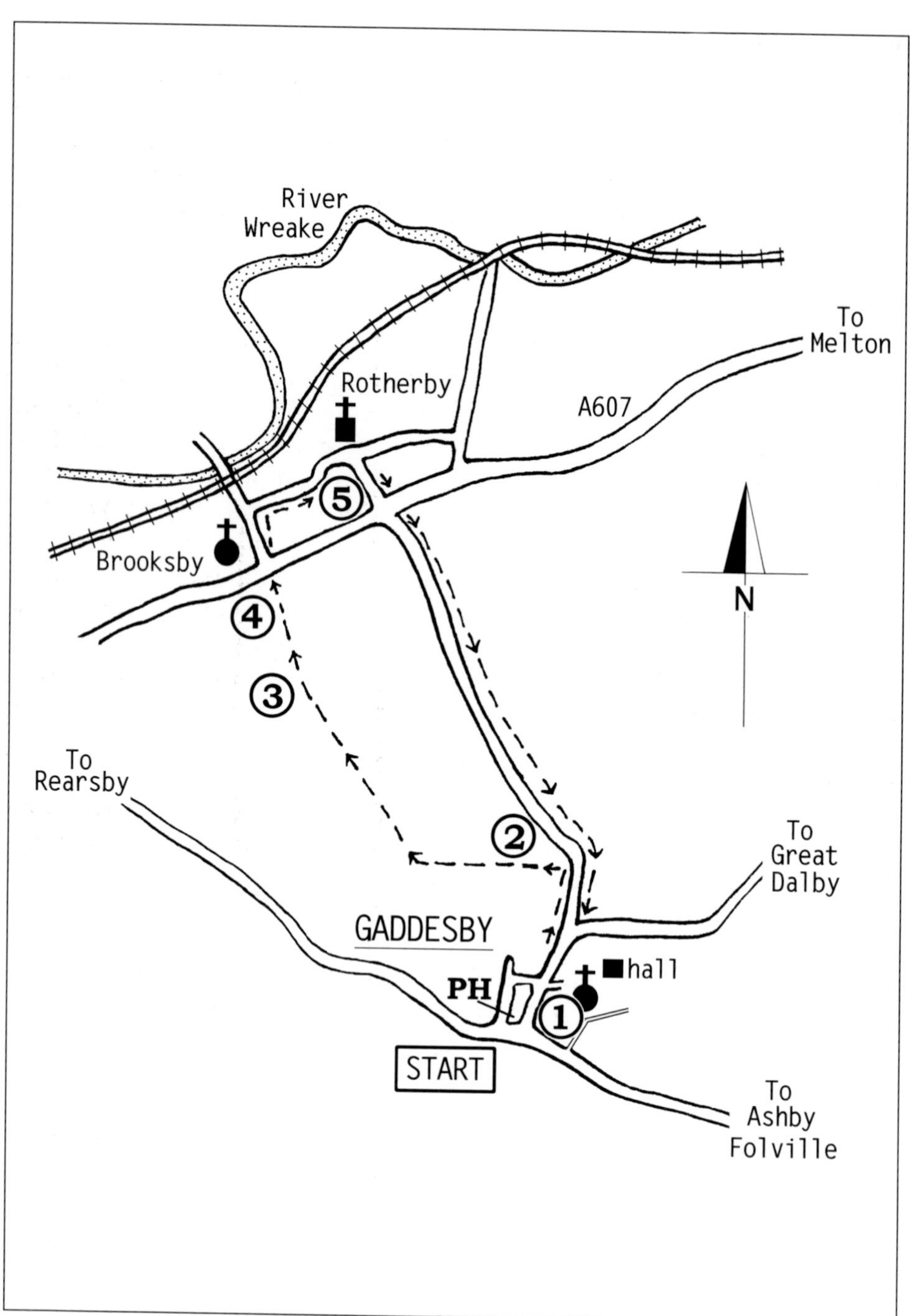
River
Wreake
To
Melton
Rotherby
A607
5
Brooksby
4
3
N
To
Rearsby
2
To
Great
Dalby
GADDESBY
hall
PH
1
START
To
Ashby
Folville

INTRODUCTION

Gaddesby is a tidy and attractive village located amidst the rolling hills of eastern Leicestershire. Our walk starts in the village then rambles over the fields to Brooksby and the river Wreake. Brooksby Hall is now an agricultural college but was once the house of Admiral Lord Beatty of Jutland. Then it's on to nearby Rotherby, and back to Gaddesby via a pleasant country lane, and to the heroic Colonel Cheney.

HISTORY

St Luke's church was described by Pevsner as 'one of the largest and most beautiful of the village churches of Leicestershire'. Nearby is the Cheney Arms and Gaddesby Hall. All three have a link, namely Colonel Edward Cheney, who lived in the Hall until his death in 1848. Inside the church is one of the most remarkable monuments in England – an almost life-size statue of a horse and rider. It commemorates Colonel Cheney, the hero of Waterloo (1815) who had four horses killed under him and a fifth wounded all within 24 hours. There are other scenes from the famous battle on the base of the statue. After a distinguished military career Colonel Cheney married a Leicestershire lady and retired to Gaddesby Hall. He became a prominent member of the hunting society in the Melton Mowbray area, and was known as 'a man of the people'.

THE PLACE

The statue, sculptured by Joseph Gott in 1848, was kept at Gaddesby Hall until 1917, when it was mounted on rollers and dragged to the church where it has remained as an unusual and outstanding attraction.

THE WALK

❶ Start at the Cheney Arms car park. Turn left into Main Street. Carry on up this street which becomes Park Hill, up to Pasture Lane. Go ahead into Rotherby Lane for about $^1/_2$ mile. Just beyond Carlton House Lodge you reach a sign on your left 'Midshires Way Bridleway to Brooksby $2^1/_2$ miles'.

❷ Go through the metal gate here and along the hedge on your right at the side of a field. Keep ahead to a gap in a fence then straight on to a metal gate at the far side of the field. This leads to a narrow path between hedges. You emerge to follow the path with trees on your left side, still walking ahead. Then keep to a wide farm track bearing right uphill. Go through a five-bar gate and across a field to a gate on the far side, then alongside a hedge and

Brooksby church

straight on. At the marker post go ahead into a farm track.

❸ The farm belongs to Brooksby Agricultural College – Spinney Farm. You have now reached the farm drive with a good surface. Follow this until you come to the main Melton-Leicester road, the A607.

❹ At the main road cross carefully into the lane opposite. Shortly you turn right into the lane leading to Rotherby. Before you do so, go left to look at Brooksby. Now you return to cross the parkland leading to Rotherby.

❺ Turn right opposite the church into Gaddesby Lane. Follow the lane uphill and in 1/4 mile you reach the A607. Again, cross carefully, then return to Gaddesby via this pleasant country lane – the distance is about 2 miles.

HOSTELRY AND THIRSTQUENCHER

The Cheney Arms (Everards) in Rearsby Lane, Gaddesby offers bar meals, real ale (Original, Tiger, Adnams bitter), Stella Artois, Scrumpy Jack, Guinness on draught and a patio garden. En-suite accommodation. Closed Tuesday am. Telephone: 01664 840260.

OTHER PLACES OF INTEREST

Brooksby Plant Centre, Brooksby College is open daily 10.30 am to 4.30 pm, the extensive gardens are open on Sundays July to September 10 am to 4 pm. Telephone: 01664 434974. Hollies Farm Handicrafts at Little Dalby, showroom and tea room: Easter to October Saturday 2 pm to 5 pm, Sunday & Bank Holidays 11 am to 5 pm.

WALK 14
JOHN CLARE: PEASANT POET AT PICKWORTH

Length: $6^1/_2$ miles

The lime kilns at Pickworth

HOW TO GET THERE: Great Casterton is just off the A1, north of Stamford.

PARKING: Sensible parking in the village and at the Crown.

MAP: OS Explorer 15 Rutland Water & Stamford (GR 002088).

INTRODUCTION

This is a lovely walk through a landscape that inspired one of our great poets – John Clare, the so-called 'Peasant Poet'. In summer, flower-edged tracks take you from the attractive village of Great Casterton, where he lived, to picturesque ruins at Pickworth, where Clare worked at the lime kiln.

HISTORY

The Napoleonic wars had just ended and there was a severe shortage of farm work. John Clare was 24 years old. He had failed to get his poems published; his parents were close to eviction due to his father's illness and he had broken

The church of St Peter and St Paul, Great Casterton

up with his childhood sweetheart, Mary Joyce. Helpston, his own Fenland village had little to offer. He heard that work lime-burning, a dirty and dangerous job, was available around Great Casterton, 8 miles away, north of Stamford. Such work attracted rough, hard-drinking characters but his need was great and the pay good. In April 1817 Clare went to work for a Mr Wilders who owned several lime kilns and the New Inn, now known as Bridge House, which you can see in Great Casterton in the first part of the walk. Clare went into lodgings in the village which he described as 'a pleasant lively town consisting of a row of houses on each side of the turnpike about a furlong long'. Then the Great North Road passed through the village. Now it bypasses it. On his day off, Sundays, he walked to the Flower Pot, Tickencote, for a drink – no longer an inn but the much-altered Flower Pot Cottage. One day he came across a pretty girl crossing nearby fields, Martha Turner, 18 year old daughter of William Turner who owned Walk Farm, now ruined and in the fields close to our walk. Eventually, Patty (as he called her) and John were married on 16th March 1820, in St Peter & St Paul's church in the village. Afterwards they crossed the road to celebrate in the Crown Inn. Both church and inn are still there on your walk.

For some time Clare's work had been at the nearby hamlet of Pickworth, 3 miles north of Great Casterton. Our walk culminates at the Pickworth lime kiln, recently restored, close by a solitary arch, the ruins of a previous church. The strange remoteness of the place led him to write his *Elegy on the Ruins of Pickworth* – 'hastily composed and written with a pencil on the spot'. Late in 1820 Clare's first volume, *Poems Descriptive of Rural Life and Scenery*, was published and he returned to Helpston. Patty eventually joined him there and their first child was born on 2nd June. He was sad to leave Rutland and 'left it with regret and rather wished to return, as I liked the farm and fields and solitudes were wild and far better than the fenny flats.' The Peasant Poet, as he became known, achieved fame and popularity until a decline after 1832. Attacks of depression sent him to an asylum in Northampton in 1841, dying in 1864. He is buried in Helpston churchyard, which is near enough for you to visit.

THE PLACE

The walk summarises Clare's time in Rutland with the church, Bridge House and Crown Inn at Great Casterton; the walk through the fields to the lime kiln at Pickworth, passing the ruin of Walk Farm. Tickencote is only 1 mile away if you wish to visit this charming tiny village.

The Crown Inn where John Clare celebrated his marriage

THE WALK

❶ Start at the Crown Inn opposite the church, turning right out of the car park. Walk along the dignified main street, once the Great North Road, until you reach the crossroads with Bridge House on the corner.

❷ Bear right into Pickworth Lane, the middle of the three roads. Carry on for about 1 mile until you reach Mounts Lodge on the right. Opposite is a Public Bridleway sign.

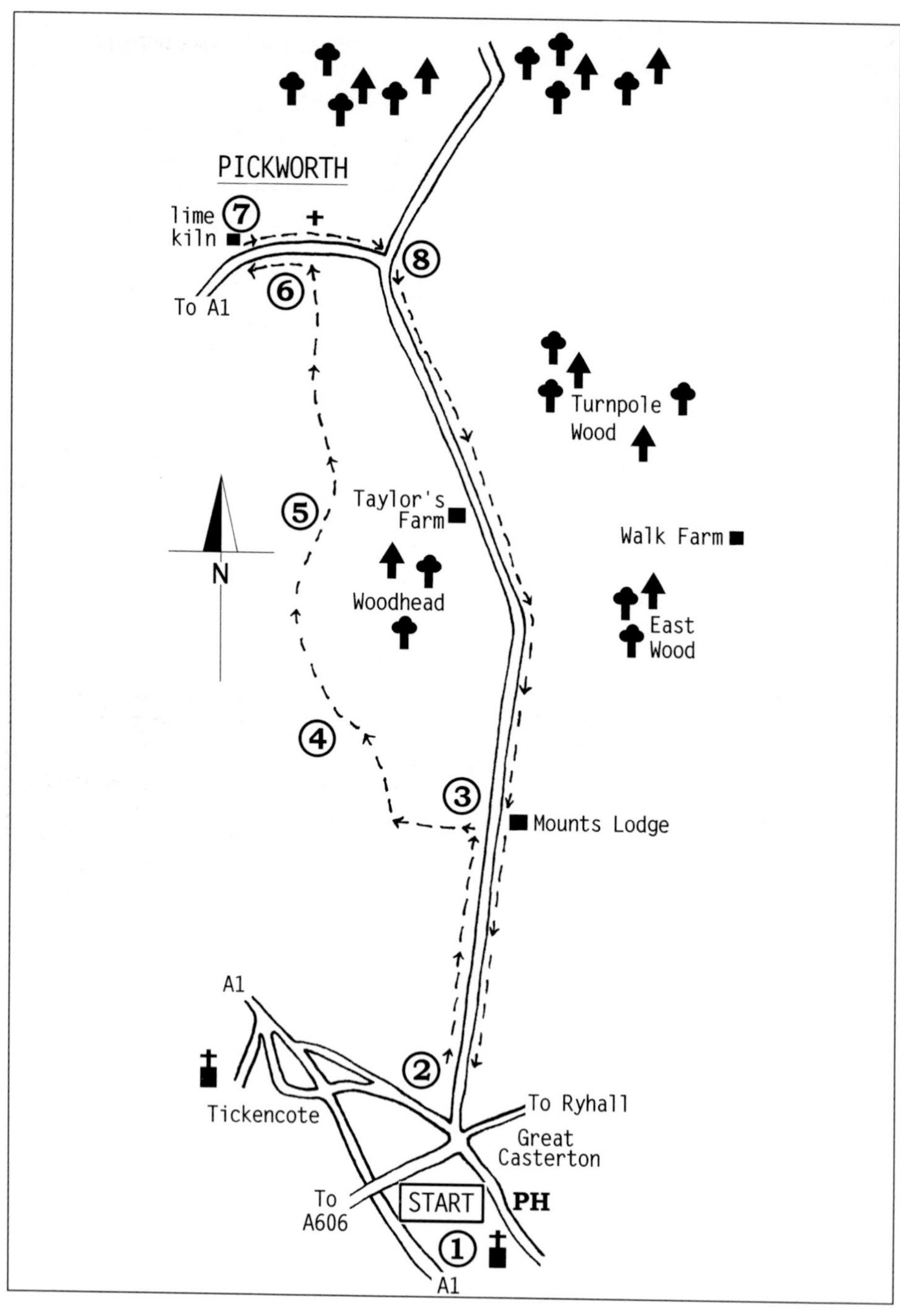
PICKWORTH
lime kiln
7
8
6
To A1
Turnpole Wood
5
Taylor's Farm
Walk Farm
N
Woodhead
East Wood
4
3
Mounts Lodge
A1
2
To Ryhall
Tickencote
Great Casterton
To A606
START
PH
1
A1

❸ Go into this bridleway on your left. In about $1/4$ mile at a marker post labelled 'Rutland Round' turn right to follow the wide and level track. There are many wild flowers here in summer. Follow yellow marker posts downhill and carry on at the signpost, do not turn right.

> **HOSTELRY AND THIRSTQUENCHER**
>
> The thatched Crown Inn at Great Casterton serves bar meals, Ashby's fine tea and coffee, and real ales. Good car park. Telephone: 01780 763362.

❹ Where the track bears left carry straight on to a marker post indicating to the left of a hedge alongside a field. This is an overgrown path. Follow marker posts looking out for one marker post which shows a half-right turn into a field leading to a gate.

❺ Go through this gate into a narrow path between hedges. Pass through another gate then straight on across fields to Pickworth, which you see ahead.

❻ At the main road, turn left for a short distance to visit John Clare's lime kiln on the right.

❼ Next, return along the road to Pickworth to the T-junction.

❽ Turn right here and follow Pickworth Lane back to Great Casterton, a distance of just over 2 miles. Opposite Taylor's Farm, on your left, you will see the path to Walk Farm, the former home of Clare's wife, 'Sweet Patty of the Vale'.

> **OTHER PLACES OF INTEREST**
>
> Great Casterton has the remains of a Roman town in a field opposite the Community College. The historic town of Stamford is only $1\frac{1}{2}$ miles to the south east. Nearby is the outstanding Burghley House open: April to October 11 am to 5 pm daily. Gardens 11 am to 4 pm daily during April. Telephone: 01780 752451.

Walk 15

Barrowden and the Founder of Modern Tourism

Length: 4 miles

Barrowden, a classic English village

HOW TO GET THERE: From the A1 follow the A47 (Leicester) or the A43 south-west from Stamford. Barrowden is ½ mile off the A47.

PARKING: Sensible parking in the village.

MAPS: OS Explorer 15 Rutland Water & Stamford (GR 951002).

INTRODUCTION

Barrowden is the pride of Rutland. It is the classic English village with a green and duck pond overlooked by the Exeter Arms; full of attractive stone buildings, a river nearby and a lovely walk to reach St Peter's church. It must be very much the same as when Thomas Cook arrived in the 1820s. The walk follows a country lane out of Barrowden and returns along the Jurassic Way, with views over the river Welland.

HISTORY

Thomas Cook was an itinerant Baptist minister, or rural missionary. In 1829 alone he walked over 2,000 miles carrying out his work. Here at Barrowden he met Marianne Mason, a farmer's daughter, who lived at West Farm in the village. She taught in the Sunday school. By 1831 the missionary funds had run out and Thomas returned to his old craft of cabinet-maker, setting up business in Barrowden. On 2nd March 1833, Thomas and Marianne were married in St Peter's, Barrowden as it was not until 1837 that marriage could take place in non-conformist chapels. Later, the couple decided to move to Market Harborough – very likely taking the road out of Barrowden to Caldecott, thence Market Harborough via the Welland valley – part of our walk. For ten years the couple lived in Market Harborough in Adam and Eve Street. One day, 9th June 1841, whilst walking from Market Harborough to Leicester, Thomas had a flash of inspiration: 'what a glorious thing it would be if the newly developed powers of railways... could be made subservient to the promotion of Temperance.' On 5th July 1841, Thomas organised the first ever day excursion by railway, from Leicester to a temperance fete at Loughborough. Thus began his travel business which led to the great firm of Thomas Cook & Son. Truly he was the 'Founder of World Tourism'.

THE PLACE

The Baptist Chapel (1819) is where Thomas preached and we go through a village much the same as 20 year old Thomas would have known it. The lane

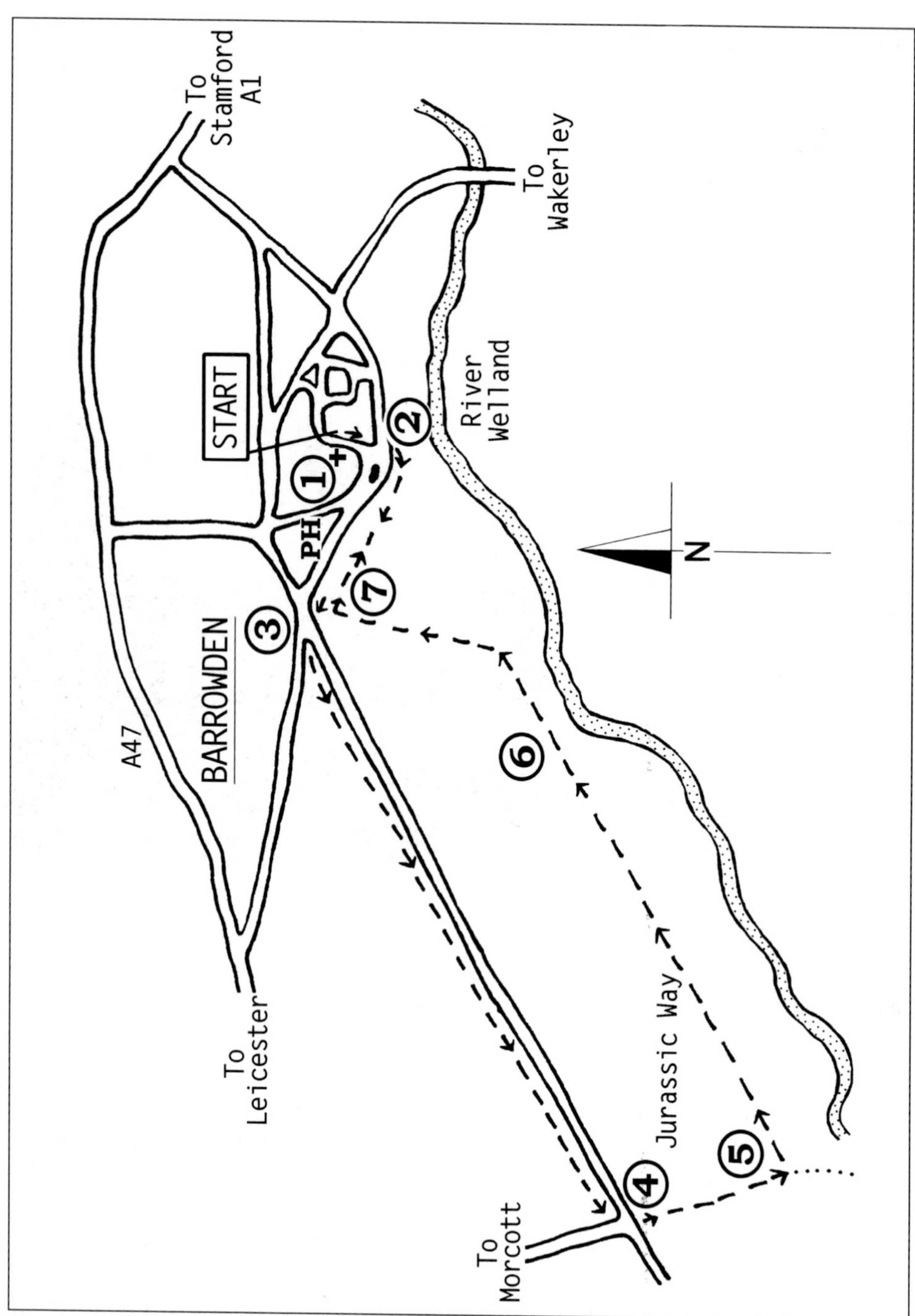
To Stamford A1
To Wakerley
River Welland
START
1
2
PH
3
7
N
BARROWDEN
A47
6
To Leicester
Jurassic Way
5
4
To Morcott

out of Barrowden is the one Thomas and his wife would follow. In the distance the Welland Viaduct reminds us of the railway revolution (though the couple would not have seen it, as it was not built until 1878).

St Peter's church, Barrowden

The Walk

❶ Start at the Baptist Chapel in Chapel Lane. Go down the lane and turn right at the Green.

❷ Carry on to the Exeter Arms and follow Main Street round until you reach the signpost to Seaton.

❸ Turn left into Seaton Road. Walk along this straight country lane for just over 1 mile. A little past Redhill Farm you reach the corner of the B672.

❹ Turn left at the sign Laxton Green Lane and walk down to and over the railway bridge (note Welland Viaduct to the right).

❺ Turn left at the yellow marker post (do not go straight on). Go through 50 yards of rough to a stile signposted 'Jurassic Way'. Follow the yellow marker over the stile along the left side of a grassy field near the hedge. Keeping left, go over the next stile and continue straight ahead. Climb over two more stiles following marker posts to the left alongside a hedge and wire fence.

❻ Turn left at a yellow marker post, crossing over a stile beside a metal gate.

Thomas Cook preached here in Barrowden

After 20 yards turn right over a stile into a field. Follow the hedge on the right-hand side (nice view of the meandering river Welland). Go straight on but bear left, as the marker post shows, diagonally across the fields over another stile into a paddock to the stile opposite.

❼ Go over the stile into a farm road, turn left then right to return to the village. Remember to go down Church Lane to see St Peter's where Thomas and Marianne were married.

HOSTELRY AND THIRSTQUENCHER

The Exeter Arms, idyllically set opposite the village green and duck pond, was formerly a 17th century coaching inn. Excellent food available every day except Monday and Sunday evening. Real ales. Car park and picnic tables outside. Telephone: 01572 747247.

OTHER PLACES OF INTEREST

Rutland Water is only 3 miles to the north. Wakerley Woods (in Northamptonshire) with forest trails and picnic sites is just over the river Welland, 1 mile away from Barrowden.

WALK 16

GEORGE STEPHENSON AND THE SWANNINGTON RAILWAY

Length: $3^1/_2$ miles

The railway lift bridge invented by George Stephenson

HOW TO GET THERE: Coalville can be reached from Junction 22 of the M1 and Junction 13 of the M42/A42 via the A511.

PARKING: At Snibston Discovery Park.

MAP: OS Landranger 129 Nottingham & Loughborough area (GR 418142).

INTRODUCTION

The exploitation of coal in north-west Leicestershire began before the 13th century and increased thereafter until the last colliery closed in 1991. The landscape bears signs of this from medieval bell-pits to the spoil heaps, old colliery sites, engine houses and disused railways visible today. At first coal was exported via pack horses, then canal and finally by rail when the Swannington to Leicester Railway opened in 1833. The famous railway engineer, George Stephenson and his son, Robert designed and built the pioneering railroad which included a notable incline. Our walk begins at Snibston Discovery Park, once Snibston No 2 colliery, passes the Stephenson Industrial Estate, over Stephenson Way to Swannington Incline then through the village, giving a fascinating glimpse of past industry and present conservation, including a nature reserve.

HISTORY

George Stephenson (1781–1848), known as the 'Father of the Railway', was born near Newcastle-upon-Tyne. For many years he gained experience with steam engines and locomotives, eventually setting up his own works and pioneering the first public passenger train between Stockton and Darlington on 27th September 1825, which he drove himself. His *Rocket* won the competition for the new Liverpool-Manchester line, which opened in 1830 using eight of Stephenson's locomotives. He continued to make improvements to steam engines, boilers and locomotives until he died in Chesterfield in 1848. His son Robert was a notable railway engineer and bridge builder. He and his father were asked by a local colliery owner, William Stenson, to design and build the Swannington Railway to exploit the concealed coalfield south of the village. The result was that Stenson opened a new colliery at Whitwick. The Stephensons also set up a mining company to develop two sites at Snibston, which led to the birth of Coalville. Other collieries were developed and, until the closure of New Lount colliery in 1969 and Bagworth in 1991, mining flourished.

THE PLACE

Today there are many reminders of the link with the Stephensons. Snibston Discovery Park is on the site of their colliery of 1832. It is appropriate that in this science and industry museum you can see galleries on local mining and take guided tours of former colliery buildings. On the walk you pass Stephenson Industrial Estate and Stephenson Way; also the site of Snibston No 3 colliery which George Stephenson's Colliery Co opened in 1850. The

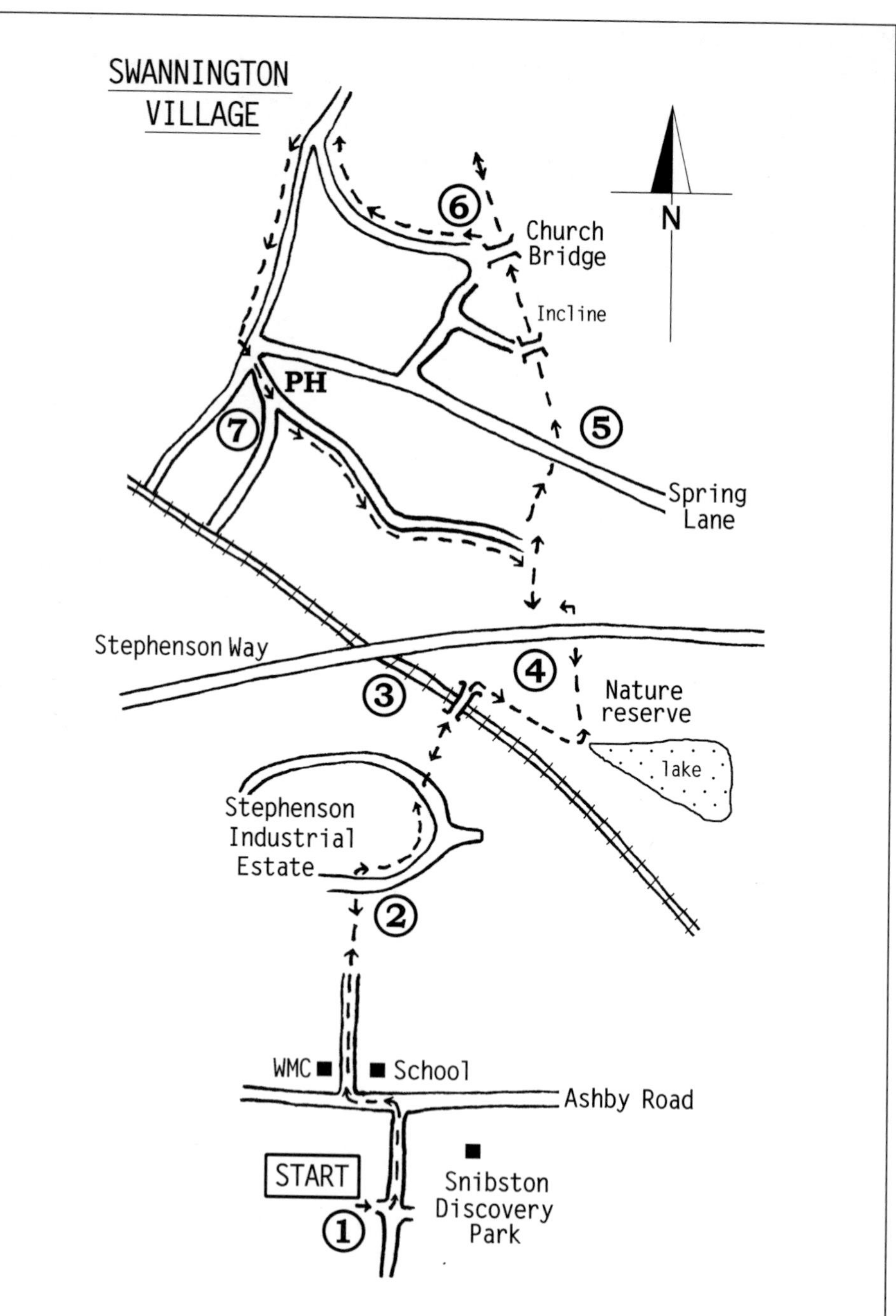
SWANNINGTON
VILLAGE
N
Church
Bridge
Incline
PH
Spring
Lane
Stephenson Way
Nature
reserve
lake
Stephenson
Industrial
Estate
WMC
School
Ashby Road
START
Snibston
Discovery
Park
1
2
3
4
5
6
7

Obsolete winding gear on the Incline, built in 1832

incline built in 1832 where coal wagons were hauled up a single track, 726 yard, 1:17 gradient by rope powered by a steam engine, is a feature of the walk. The system worked for 115 years and the original steam engine is now in the National Railway Museum, York. Snibston Discovery Park, Ashby Road, Coalville is open April to August daily 10 am to 6 pm, September to March daily 10 am to 5 pm. Telephone: 01530 510851.

THE WALK

HOSTELRY AND THIRSTQUENCHER

There is a café at Snibston Discovery Park. The Robin Hood Inn, Station Hill, is on the walk. Telephone: 01530 834398.

❶ Start at the Snibston Discovery car park. Turn left out of the park exit and walk to the A50 Ashby Road. Turn left and cross the road to Coalville Primary School opposite. In about 20 yards turn right between the school and the Working Men's Club. Go ahead down a wide lane, which soon becomes a rough path through wasteland.

❷ You arrive at the Stephenson Industrial Estate. Turn right to follow the estate road round the bend as far as Ashby Scientific Ltd on your right where you take the path on your right leading to a pedestrian railway bridge. Most of the markers are missing along this part of the route.

❸ Cross over the bridge and bear right to follow a rough path to the Nature Reserve. Continue bearing right until you cross a walkway above the edge of a lake. Then keep to the left pathway passing stiles until you reach the busy Stephenson Way (sign).

❹ Cross the road carefully to the opposite side. Go down the road bank, turn left along a rough grass path to the second stile on your right. Here signs show the way. Cross the stile and follow the path. As the path forks go ahead up a bank to a marker post at the top. Carry on ahead through rough pasture over a stile and in 50 yards to Spring Lane. Here, note the information board and wheel.

❺ Cross the lane to join the path opposite which is the site of the Swannington railway 'one of the world's earliest lines'. You now have a very pleasant walk down the Swannington Incline passing the former Engine House site, then under Potato Lane footbridge, for almost ½ mile until you reach the recently restored Church Lane Bridge. There are information boards along the route. You can carry on for 300 yards following the Incline but you will have to return to Church Lane Bridge, where, on the west side, you will find steps to take you up to the road.

❻ Turn right here to follow the road to Swannington village. At Main Street turn left and walk along until you reach the Robin Hood pub (if you want to look at the village turn right, but then return and go on to the pub).

❼ Go down Green Lane which is on the right as you face the pub. Take the

OTHER PLACES OF INTEREST

Ashby de la Zouch castle, the Moira Furnace and Craft Workshops and the National Forest Visitor Centre (see Walks 2 and 12 for details) are about 7 miles to the west. The lovely scenery of Charnwood Forest and Bradgate Park the same distance south-east.

left fork ignoring stiles to left or right. Bear left as the path continues and in ½ mile you join your original route. Take the path half-right to Stephenson Way. Once across go into the Nature Reserve on the grass path opposite, turn first right, cross a footbridge and along the raised walkway back to the railway bridge. Once over, turn left; follow the estate road round to the rough lane on the left, which leads you to Ashby Road and back to Snibston Discovery Park.

Walk 17
Edward Thring at Uppingham: A Great Headmaster

Length: 2 miles

The cricket pavilion, Uppingham school

HOW TO GET THERE: The A6003 from Melton Mowbray and Oakham passes through Uppingham to Corby.

PARKING: Some street parking may be possible but there is a free car park on North Street East.

MAPS: OS Explorer 15 Rutland Water & Stamford (GR 867996). There is a town map in the Rutland 2000 Visitor Guide (free from Tourist Centre).

INTRODUCTION

A short and easy stroll around the attractive town of Uppingham, tracing the history of the great public school and the influence of its founder, Edward Thring.

HISTORY

The Old School in the churchyard of St Peter & St Paul, Uppingham, built in 1584, is the precursor of the great public school we see all around the town today. Close by is the memorial 'erected to the memory of a beloved teacher by those of his boys who were at Uppingham October 22nd, 1887'. The teacher and headmaster was Edward Thring who came to Uppingham School in 1853 when he was 32 years of age. In ten years he increased the numbers from a handful of boys to 200 then 300 in 1865 and turned an obscure grammar school into a leading public school. Here he found his vocation. As a man of vision with strong opinions he became a pioneer in education, introducing to Uppingham many principles now accepted as normal practice. He made provision for practical activities outside the traditional range of classical studies and gave high value to music. He had a liberal and humane approach to boarding education and further education for girls, and encouraged links between town and gown. He believed that education must be concerned with the whole of human experience and he created a community which would enable body, mind and spirit to advance together. He wrote many influential educational works and was the founder of the Headmasters' Conference, which first met in Uppingham in 1869. He also established the first Mission to the Poor of London, the North Woolwich Settlement (1869).

THE PLACE

One man made Uppingham School great. Much building took place after his death in 1887 and continues at the present time. Countless innovations and many people continue to make this one of England's great schools known the world over. The character of the town has been greatly influenced by the school. Afternoon tours of Uppingham School take place from mid-June to the end of September at 2.15 pm

HOSTELRY AND THIRSTQUENCHER

Baines Tea Shop, High Street West for morning coffee, light snacks, lunch and afternoon tea. Telephone: 01572 823317. Hackneys Bistro, 6 Printers Yard, High Street East for lunch and evening meals. Telephone: 01572 822088. The Falcon Hotel is a former coaching inn overlooking the Market Place. Telephone: 01572 823535.

Victoria Tower, the fine gateway to the school

on Saturdays, 5.15 pm on Wednesdays from the Market Place. Telephone: 01572 822672/822216. There are events all year at Uppingham School Theatre, Stockerston Road, which the public can attend. Telephone: 01572 823318.

THE WALK

❶ Start at the church porch of St Peter & St Paul in the Market Place. Turn right and go round the east end of the church. The Old School, the original Uppingham School, is on your left. Turn left alongside the School then down the path and steps on your right into South Street.

❷ You reach the churchyard on your right. Go through the gate and on your left you see the memorial to Edward Thring. Return to the road. Carry on a little way to the busy London Road. Cross carefully then turn right uphill until you reach Leamington Terrace on your left.

❸ Go into this lane and as you reach a school gate, if you turn right you can follow a narrow path round the perimeter of the School. This brings you to School Lane where you can peep into the School quadrangle. From School Lane you can see the original Old Studies and Hospital of the school (1780–1814); the newer library (1949); half-right is the School Chapel (1863–65) with Thring's statue outside. Close by is the Great Hall (1923–28).

❹ Now go down School Lane to High Street West. Turn left to follow the grim, prison-like exterior of the School. You soon reach a fine gateway called Victoria Tower (1894–97) where, once again, you can see beyond. The architect, Sir Thomas Jackson, did a great deal to convey a college atmosphere to the school. Proceed up the High Street and into Stockerston Road to Uppingham School Theatre. You will see staff houses and boarding houses en route.

❺ From the Theatre return back down Stockerston Road and turn right into Spring Backway. The school playing fields are believed to be the largest in the country. Carry on to London Road.

❻ Cross the road into South Street.

OTHER PLACES OF INTEREST

Lyddington Bede House (English Heritage) is 2 miles to the south. Open daily April to October 10 am to 6 pm (5 pm in October), closed 1 pm to 2 pm. Rockingham Castle, 450 years a Royal castle, 450 years a family home, is on the A6003 4 miles south of Uppingham. Open Easter Sunday to October 1 pm to 5 pm Sundays and Thursdays; plus Tuesdays in August. Telephone: 01536 770240.

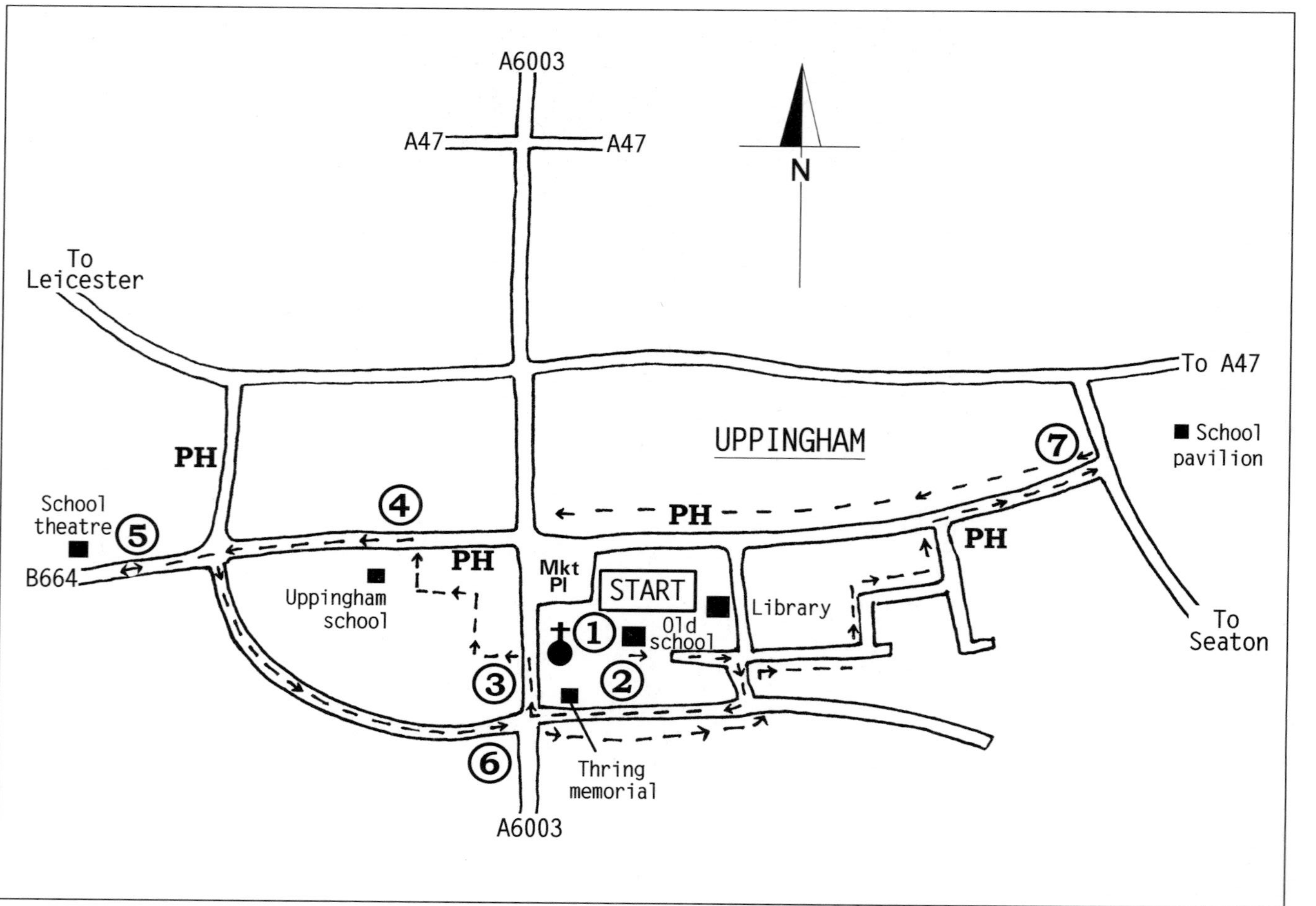
A6003
A47
A47
N
To Leicester
To A47
UPPINGHAM
7
School pavilion
PH
School theatre
5
4
PH
PH
B664
PH
Mkt Pl
START
Library
Uppingham school
1
Old school
To Seaton
3
2
6
Thring memorial
A6003

Turn left into Queen Street and Norton Street. This leads to Adderley Street and High Street East. At the Wagon and Horses, on the corner, turn right and go all the way to the end of High Street East to see the famous thatched School cricket pavilion.

❼ Now return down High Street East back to the Market Place and your starting point.

Edward Thring's statue

WALK 18
THE WELLAND VIADUCT: AN ENGINEERING MIRACLE

Length: 4 miles

The Welland viaduct marches across the Welland valley

HOW TO GET THERE: Seaton is 2½ miles east of Uppingham and the A6003. It is 1½ miles south of Glaston and the A47.

PARKING: Sensible parking in the village.

MAP: OS Explorer 15 Rutland Water & Stamford (GR 904983).

INTRODUCTION

A walk which focuses on a Victorian marvel, the incredible Welland railway viaduct. Our walk crosses the fields from Seaton to Harringworth then passes through the village, close to the river Welland. We head back to Seaton with views of the viaduct all the way, indeed we pass beneath an arch following the country lane to that village.

HISTORY

On a misty morning in the Welland valley or in the dim twilight of a sultry summer's eventide you may receive a sudden surprise as you walk from Seaton in Rutland to Harringworth in Northamptonshire. Surely that isn't a Roman aqueduct across the valley? We know Rutland is remarkable but can it compare with Nîmes? Yet as you draw nearer you can certainly discern something of a minor wonder. From Harringworth towards Seaton for three quarters of a mile, with 82 arches, each 60 feet high, there exists a brick built railway viaduct which, in its time, must have ranked as an engineering miracle of Victorian England. Built between 1876 and 1878 it carried the LMS Kettering to Manton branch line and represents the peak of railway achievement in the area. It is the longest masonry viaduct in Britain. It contains 20 million bricks, made locally. Three thousand five hundred men worked on it and were housed in shanty towns at Seaton and Gretton. It was the motorway of its time with just as much impact on the people and environment. If plans to reopen Corby station materialise then soon the famous viaduct will again take daily passenger services over its monumental arches.

THE PLACE

Who could believe that a man-made object could do so much to enhance the pastoral Welland valley? It is comforting to know that not all man's technological revolutions result in ugly effects. Far from it, as we are now just beginning to appreciate the charm and nostalgia of railway architecture.

HOSTELRY AND THIRSTQUENCHER

Excellent food and real ales at the George and Dragon, Main Street, Seaton. Telephone: 01572 747773. Also the White Swan, Seaton Road, Harringworth serves good home-cooked food and real ales. Telephone: 01572 747543. Both pubs are on your walking route.

THE WALK

❶ Go down Church Lane and turn left at the footpath sign. Then along a grass path in front of a cottage to a stile (arrow). Go over

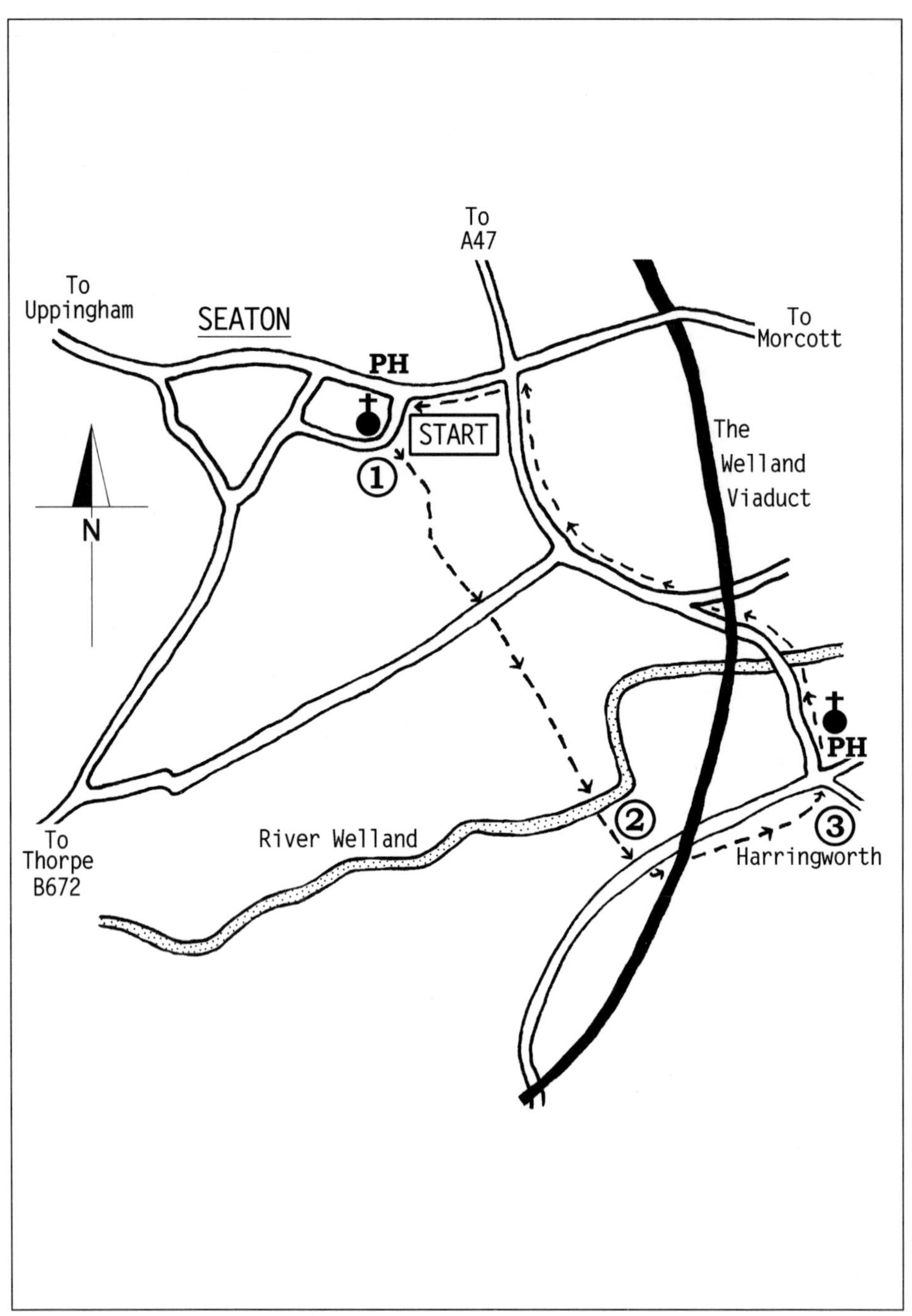
To
A47
To
Uppingham
SEATON
To
Morcott
PH
START
1
The
Welland
Viaduct
N
PH
2
3
To
Thorpe
B672
River Welland
Harringworth

The White Swan at Harringworth

the stile and alongside a fence on your left-hand side, then ahead to a marker post and stile. Now go diagonally left across a field towards the viaduct, then ahead to a marker post at an old railway embankment. Go up the steps to the top of the embankment and down the other side to a lane. Go through the gate here; turn right to a footpath sign. Cross the road to follow the sign down a farm track. Keep left around the farmhouse, then right over a footbridge. Once across go left over stiles, crossing the middle of the field towards the end of the viaduct, in the distance. At the far side, cross the footbridge and stile, go across the field to a gate on the opposite side, again in line with the right-hand side of the viaduct.

❷ Here cross the bridge over the river Welland and go through the metal gate. Go ahead to the right-hand corner of the field. At the road turn left to follow it into Harringworth.

❸ At the White Swan, turn left into Seaton Road. This takes you back to Seaton in 1½ miles, under the arches of the viaduct, and across the river Welland. As you turn right uphill to Seaton on the last ½ mile you will see the remnants of the old railway station on your right at the road junction. Turn left at the sign at the top of the hill to return to Seaton village.

OTHER PLACES OF INTEREST

Kirby Hall (English Heritage) is an impressive shell of an Elizabethan mansion with fine gardens and peacocks. Telephone: 01536 203230. Nearby is Deene Park, former home of Lord Cardigan, leader of the Charge of the Light Brigade. Telephone: 01780 450223. Both places are only 5 miles south.

Walk 19
Painting the Town Red: Melton Mowbray

Length: 3 miles

The Carnegie Museum at the start of the route

HOW TO GET THERE: Take the A606 from Nottingham; the A607 from Leicester and the same road from Grantham and the A1. From Stamford and the A1 follow the A606.

PARKING: There are many pay and display car parks, also street parking near to the Carnegie Museum.

MAPS: OS Landranger 129 Nottingham & Loughborough area (GR 757191). Free town maps are available from Melton Carnegie Museum Tourist Information Centre. Telephone: 01664 480992.

INTRODUCTION

There is so much to enjoy on this stroll around historic Melton Mowbray, recalling the places and people – and food! – that make this old market town special. The walk follows the route taken by a rowdy group one night in 1837, whose antics gave rise to a popular expression.

HISTORY

Melton Mowbray was the premier centre for fox-hunting throughout the 19th century until the 1930s. Royalty and aristocrats thronged the town in season. Usually they owned large houses, known as 'Hunting Boxes' or if they were bachelors they would resort to the Old Club in Burton Street where they would have apartments. One of the most infamous events in the history of fox-hunting took place on 6th April 1837. After a day's hunting and a night's drinking at a Hunt Ball, the Marquis of Waterford and his friends ran riot through the town. They barricaded the toll-keeper in his house at Thorpe End, then went down Sherrard Street into the market square, Church Street and King Street painting doors, shop fronts and even people – *red*! Local constables who challenged them were also painted. Thus was born the world famous expression, 'painting the town red'.

THE PLACE

Today there is still a great deal to see as a legacy of the great era of hunting. Our walk starts at the Carnegie Museum, Thorpe End, where there are displays and information relating to the sport, also some of John Ferneley's famous paintings of horses and hunting. Tuesday is a prime day to visit the Cattle Market; Friday is the Farmer's Market; Tuesday, Wednesday and Saturday there are street markets.

THE WALK

❶ Start at the Carnegie Museum, Thorpe End. Go left into town via Sherrard Street to the Market Place.

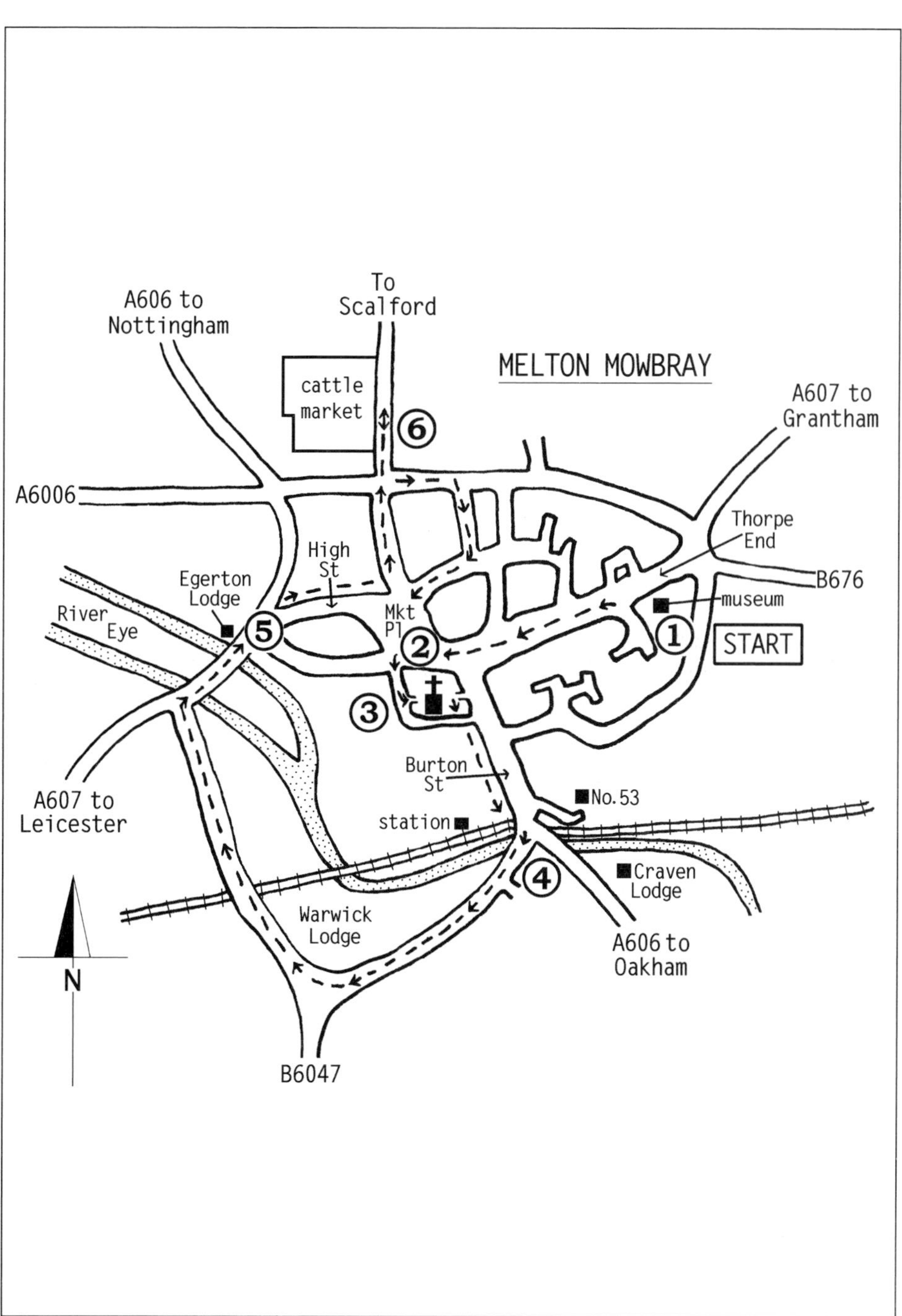
MELTON MOWBRAY
To Scalford
A606 to Nottingham
cattle market
A607 to Grantham
A6006
Thorpe End
B676
museum
START
High St
Egerton Lodge
Mkt Pl
River Eye
Burton St
No. 53
station
A607 to Leicester
Craven Lodge
Warwick Lodge
A606 to Oakham
B6047
N
1
2
3
4
5
6

Egleton Lodge, once a focal point of the hunting high society

❷ Go round the Butter Cross then into Church Street. On your left look up to see the White Swan sign. Here the 'Mad Marquis' was lifted up to paint the Swan. Carry on to St Mary's church to see the memorial to John Ferneley.

❸ As you emerge from the church turn right to follow the path into Burton Street, where opposite the church, the Old Club was located. In this street was Coventry House, the lodge of the Earl of Coventry; Lord Carrington's Manor House (No 27) and just past the Harborough Hotel & Ferry Boat Inn, the Earl of Cardigan's Brudenell House (No 53). Of course, the railway station was convenient to these 'Boxes'. Turn right and go down to Burton Bridge. Bear

The White Swan which was painted red

left to see Craven Lodge – now a Special School – where the Prince of Wales, later Duke of Windsor, stayed, often walking up Ankle Hill to Warwick Lodge to meet the Duke of Gloucester after breakfast.

❹ Return and turn left into Ankle Hill. Ascend Warwick Road. Turn right down Dalby Road. Along this road Mowbray Lodge and the Lodge were located. At the junction with Leicester Road turn right and cross Lady Wilton's bridge. Egerton Lodge is on your left, once home of the Earl and Countess of Wilton and a focal point for hunting high society with many famous visitors, including King Edward VII when he was Prince of Wales in 1873.

❺ Now cross via traffic lights into the High Street. Here is the town's oldest surviving coaching inn, the George, and opposite on the site of the HSBC Bank, the New Club was located. Turning left at the Corn Cross into Nottingham Street you see *Ye Olde Pork Pie Shoppe*, a reminder that pork pies were 'popular with the hunting fraternity', as were the famous Hunt Cakes. Stilton cheese produced in the area was also much in demand. Cross over Norman Way into Scalford Road opposite. Turn left into the Cattle Market. The Cattle Market, especially the

HOSTELRY AND THIRSTQUENCHER

There is a wonderful variety of pubs, hotels and cafes in Melton, all near the town centre. Two places with character are the Grapes, Church Street, and the Anne of Cleves, Burton Street.

Horse & Tack Auctions on the first Saturday in each month, is part of the context of hunting. Opposite the entrance John Ferneley's former home, Elgin Lodge, was sited until demolished in 1982. A little further up Scalford Road was Lord Newport's Lodge. In the great era of hunting the town was full of hunting boxes, which are now either much altered or demolished.

OTHER PLACES OF INTEREST

Waterfield Leisure Park, telephone: 01664 563550. Melton Country Park has 140 acres of parkland and a lake, picnic sites, trails and play areas. Open all year. Telephone: 01664 480164. Melton Theatre Leisure Centre, telephone: 01664 850850. Indoor and outdoor bowling with restaurant and bar, telephone: 01664 410159. Tumbledown Farm, Spinney Road, Melton Mowbray is a working farm, licensed farmhouse kitchen, gifts, hatchery, poultry, rare breeds, crafts, pets, milking parlour, trails and play areas. Telephone: 01664 481811. Belvoir Castle, telephone: 01476 870262.

❻ On emerging, turn right, then left into Norman Way. Cross over to St Mary's Way, into King Street and back to the Market Place. Turn left along Sherrard Street to return to the start.

Walk 20
The Prince of Wales and Mrs Simpson at Burrough

Length: $3^1/_2$ miles

The Bower House where a romance blossomed

HOW TO GET THERE: From Melton Mowbray take the B6047 to Great Dalby then follow signs to Burrough.

PARKING: Sensible parking in the village.

MAP: OS Landranger 129 Nottingham & Loughborough and 141 Kettering & Corby (GR 758109).

INTRODUCTION

Burrough-on-the-Hill is a remote village situated in the rolling hills of High Leicestershire, 6 miles south of Melton Mowbray. It is well-known for its Iron Age hill fort and for the outstanding fox-hunting country around. However, this obscure village entered the annals of history when, in the autumn of 1930, Edward, Prince of Wales, was introduced to Mrs Wallis Simpson at Burrough Court House. The walk explores this 'Royal' village and passes Burrough Court Farm and the site of Burrough Court, all set in wonderful scenery.

HISTORY

Burrough Court was situated a little to the south of the village. Built in 1905 it was accidentally burnt down in 1944, only the outbuildings being left. In the 1920s and 30s it was owned by Viscount Furness – Marmaduke 'Duke' Furness, the shipping magnate. Both Duke and his wife Thelma (especially Thelma) were good friends of the Prince and so he was a frequent visitor, hunting from Burrough Court on many occasions. Of course, the Prince had become a regular of the hunting set in Melton by 1923. He was regarded by all as a gentleman, popular with all classes of society. As a rider he showed 'reckless bravado... being easily unseated'. He was often seen round and about as 'he used to go out quite a lot, just get into his car with no equerry or anyone to look after him'. Once they had met, the Prince and Mrs Simpson frequently visited Burrough Court. Much of the early romance blossomed in the thatched Bower House in a wood at the house. A telephone was installed to link with the main house. It was here that the firm relationship developed which led to the abdication in 1936.

THE PLACE

The Bower House was moved into the garden at Burrough House in the village, where it is occasionally open to the public. It is seen most often by people attending weddings, conferences and concerts organised by Burrough House Enterprises. Indeed, couples can be married in the Bower House. Near the village is the 'airfield' where planes landed bringing guests in the 1930s. The Prince must have walked round the village from time to time and worshipped at the 13th century St Mary's. Certainly, he often visited the post office in nearby Somerby and the inn at Twyford. He is reported to have been pushed around the grounds of Burrough Court in a pram – by Wallis and Thelma – during evening festivities. Did they ever picnic on Burrough Hill?

The former hangar used by the Prince of Wales in the 1930s

THE WALK

❶ Start at the church. Walk down Main Street towards Burrough House. Turn left here into a narrow country lane leading to Newbold. As you walk along the lane you have expansive views all around. You proceed downhill and in 1 mile from Burrough you reach Newbold Grange Farm.

HOSTELRY AND THIRSTQUENCHER

The Stag & Hounds, Main Street, has healthy and excellent food with plenty of atmosphere. Telephone: 01664 454181. Also, in nearby Somerby is the 16th century Stilton Cheese Inn with great food and real ales seven days a week, menu and daily specials. Telephone: 01664 454394. The Old Brewery, Somerby, is famous for the strongest beer in the world, Baz's Bonce Blower. Visits to the brewery (day and evening). Telephone: 01664 454777.

❷ On your right, just before the farm drive, there is a bridlepath sign. Go into the field, as directed, keeping to the fence on your left-hand side. Go through a wooden

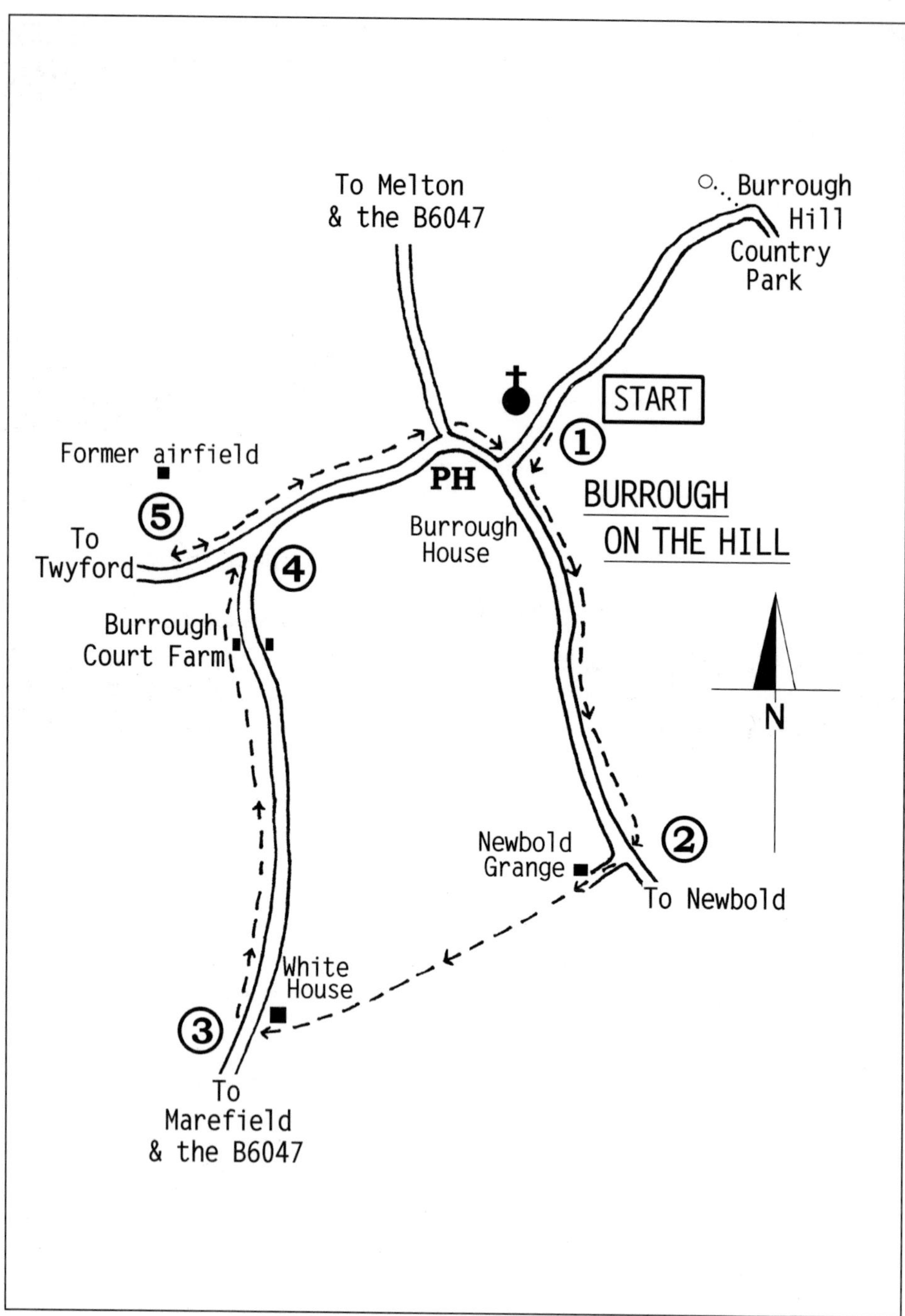
To Melton
& the B6047
Burrough
Hill
Country
Park
START
1
PH
Former airfield
5
To
Twyford
4
Burrough
House
BURROUGH
ON THE HILL
N
Burrough
Court Farm
Newbold
Grange
2
To Newbold
White
House
3
To
Marefield
& the B6047

farm gate into a narrow paddock between a hedge on the left and a fence on the right. Then go ahead to a white metal gate, bear left through a farmyard to another metal gate to the left of a large barn. Go right to a small wooden gate 10 yards away, then left alongside a hedge to the far corner of the field. Through a gate and alongside a fence to the far corner. Then over a concrete bridge with double gates. Bear right round the field edge along a wide grassy track to the marker post at the far corner. Go through a narrow metal gate bearing right alongside the hedge to a wooden gate next to a sign and marker post at the far right corner. Here you emerge onto a country lane at White House Farm.

OTHER PLACES OF INTEREST

Burrough Hill Iron Age fort, 700 feet above sea level, is 1½ miles north-east of the village: car park and toilets, picnics and walks. Hollies Farm Handicrafts, at Little Dalby sells quality furniture and has a tea-shop with home-made cakes. Telephone: 01664 454553.

❸ Turn right and follow the country lane back 1 mile to the main road.

❹ Turn left at the main road and walk for about 500 yards when you reach the drive into Burrough Court Estates. This is the drive into the former Burrough Court House. If you look into the field opposite you will see the hangar, which was on the small airfield in the 1930s.

❺ Now turn back along the road and return to the village.

SOME SUGGESTED READING

Baker, Denis, *Swannington Village Trail*, Swannington Heritage Trust

Brownlow, Jack, *Melton Mowbray, Queen of the Shires*, Sycamore Press, 1980

Cantor, Leonard and Squires, Anthony, *The Historic Parks and Gardens of Leicestershire & Rutland*, Kairos Press, 1997

Cantor, Leonard, *The Historic Country Houses of Leicestershire & Rutland*, Kairos Press, 1998

Clough, T.H.McK., 'Peter de Neville and his wrong doing as Warden of the Forest of Rutland', *Rutland Record* no. 18, 1998

Hartley, F, *Medieval Earthworks of Rutland*, Leicestershire Museums, 1983

Keene, Barbara, *The Bower House: memories of the Duke of Windsor and Wallis Simpson* (video 40 mins. Telephone: 01572 787459)

Kington, John, *The Weather Journals of a Rutland Squire*, Rutland Record Society, 1988

Laughton, Mike, *The Welland Viaduct*, Rutland Magazine Feb/April 2000

Lee, Joyce, *Who's Buried Where in Leicestershire*, Leicestershire Libraries & Information, 1991

Lines, Rodney, 'John Clare's Rutland', *Rutland Record* no. 13, 1993

Mayhew, Charles Revd., *Lyndon Rutland: a guide*, Rutland Local History & Record Society Occ. Pub. no. 5, 1999

Mining Heritage Trail: North-West Leicestershire, Leicester County Council

Moira Trail, Leicestershire Industrial History Society

Scott, Sir Walter, *Ivanhoe*, 1819

Squires, Anthony, 'Flitteris & Cold Overton: Two Medieval Deer Parks' *Rutland Record* no. 12, 1992

Tibble, J.W. and Anne, *John Clare Selected Poems*, Everyman Library, Dent, 1965, 1975

Tozer, Malcolm, 'The Great Educational Experiment Edward Thring at Uppingham School' *Rutland Record* no. 12, 1992

Whitelaw, Jeffery W., *Hidden Leicestershire & Rutland*, Countryside Books, 1996

Waites, Bryan (ed), 'Who Was Who in Rutland', *Rutland Record* no. 8, 1987

Waites, Bryan (ed), *Celebration of Rutland*, Multum in Parvo Press, 1994